The Actor, Image, and Action

D1595345

'Valuable and provocative insight in an area of thinking that is still relatively new to the field of theatre . . . Rhonda Blair's work has the potential to lead toward new techniques in actor training'

Sharon Carnicke, *University of Southern California*

The Actor, Image, and Action is a 'new generation' approach to the craft of acting; the first full-length study of actor training using the insights of cognitive neuroscience. In a brilliant reassessment of both the practice and theory of acting, Rhonda Blair examines the physiological relationship between bodily action and emotional experience. In doing so she provides the latest step in Stanislavski's attempts to help the actor 'reach the unconscious by conscious means'.

Recent developments in scientific thinking about the connections between biology and cognition require new ways of understanding many elements of human activity, including:

- imagination
- emotion
- memory
- physicality
- reason.

The Actor, Image, and Action looks at how these are in fact inseparable in the brain's structure and function, and their crucial importance to an actor's engagement with a role. The book vastly improves our understanding of the actor's process and is a must for any actor or student of acting.

Rhonda Blair is Professor of Theatre at Southern Methodist University. Her writings on acting and cognitive neuroscience appear in journals such as *Theatre Topics* and collections such as *Performance and Cognition: Theatre Studies and the Cognitive Turn*.

The Actor, Image, and Action

Acting and Cognitive Neuroscience

Rhonda Blair

Routledge
Taylor & Francis Group

LONDON AND NEW YORK

First published 2008
by Routledge
2 Park Square, Milton Park, Abingdon, Oxon OX14 4RN

Simultaneously published in the USA and Canada
by Routledge
270 Madison Ave, New York, NY 10016

Routledge is an imprint of the Taylor & Francis Group, an informa business

Typeset in Sabon by
Florence Production Ltd, Stoodleigh, Devon
Printed and bound in Great Britain by
MPG Books Ltd, Bodmin, Cornwall

British Library Cataloguing in Publication Data
A catalogue record for this book is available from the British Library

Library of Congress Cataloging in Publication Data
Blair, Rhonda, 1951–
    The actor, image, and action : acting and cognitive
neuroscience / by Rhonda Blair.
        p. cm.
        Includes bibliographical references and index.
    1. Acting—Psychological aspects.   2. Cognitive neuroscience.
I. Title.
PN2058.B56 2008
792.02′8—dc22   2007022532

ISBN10: 0–415–77416–0 (hbk)
ISBN10: 0–415–77417–9 (pbk)
ISBN10: 0–203–93810–0 (ebk)

ISBN13: 978–0–415–77416–1 (hbk)
ISBN13: 978–0–415–77417–8 (pbk)
ISBN13: 978–0–203–93810–2 (ebk)

For Bill and my students

Contents

Acknowledgments

This project is the result of experiences in performing, directing, reading, and teaching, and of conversations with numerous colleagues. I have been informed by the writing of Joseph Roach and Sharon Carnicke, who provided ways of thinking about acting and science and about Stanislavsky, respectively, that are fundamental to this book. Colleagues, especially Bruce McConachie, John Lutterbie, Amy Cook, Sarah Barker, John Emigh, Mark Pizzato, F. Elizabeth Hart, Andrew Sofer, J. Ellen Gainor, Phil Auslander, Kiki Gounaridou, Alan Brown, Tom Postlewaite, Carol Sorgenfrei, Tracy Davis, Gay Cima, and John Gronbeck-Tedesco provided sounding boards for earlier versions of this work. I am not sure I would have pursued this research as I have without encountering some of my colleagues at Southern Methodist University; most particularly, Michael Connolly has been a valuable fellow traveler, talking with me about the implications of the science and discussing applications in his acting classes and rehearsals. My thanks always to the Department of Theatre and Film at the University of Kansas for providing me, decades ago, with an education that refused to separate theory and practice, in particular to Ron Willis for helping me to think about theory, history, and theatre in a way that was transforming; Jack Wright, for his guidance and wisdom as a director and coach; Bill Kuhlke, for deepening my appreciation for Stanislavsky and Chekhov; and Gerald Mikkelson, for making it possible for me to work with Russian texts and actually to get to Moscow. Colleagues at Hampshire College, especially Ellen Donkin, Becky Nordstrom, and Wayne Kramer, provided a school in thinking interdisciplinarily. The Division of Theatre, the Meadows School of the Arts, and the University Research Council of Southern Methodist University provided funds for conference travel. Earlier versions of some of the material in this book appeared in *Performance and Cognition: Theatre Studies and the Cognitive Turn* (2006: 167–185), *Method Acting Reconsidered: Theory, Practice, Future* (2000: 201–218), *Metamorphosis* (2001: 148–164), and *Theatre Topics* (12:2, September 2002: 177–190). Dallas's feminist Echo Theatre, particularly Pam Myers-Morgan, Ellen Locy, and Terry Ferguson, provided me with a gifted community of theatre professionals with whom to work on this material. Many thanks to my students at SMU, with whom I've explored these issues in classes and rehearsals, especially to MFA acting students who have formally considered and discussed this material with me and to David Matherly. LeAnn Field was central in initiating this project. I deeply appreciate Talia Rodgers's and Minh Ha Duong's great work in helping this book reach print. Finally, my deep and joyful thanks to my partner Bill Beach, without whose support, patience, and excellent cooking this book might not have come to fruition.

Preface

In 1906, Konstantin Stanislavsky, the father of modern acting, felt stuck—unable to find a passionate connection that he could consistently tap into when playing a role. So he began reading voraciously, including the work of research psychologists such as Théodule Ribot, William James, and Carl Lange, to see if the science might be taken into the studio. For the next thirty years, among other things, applying science to acting was what he did. Throughout his mature career, Stanislavsky was committed to exploring the possibilities for science's utility in the service of tapping into the mystery of acting.

Like many of us, I'm a hybrid: director, performer, and academic writer. Like many of us, I have been frustrated by the fissures and places of resistance in discussions of the relationship between practice and theory. There is the unnecessary mystification and anti-intellectualism in some writing and talking about the actor's process by practitioners, and approaches to and beliefs about acting that keep us "small" and constrain our imaginations. There is the sometimes blanket skepticism about narrative, feeling, or science in what are otherwise useful postmodern theories (this seems to me to be a kind of neo-Cartesianism, or what feminist cognitive neuro-scientist Elizabeth Wilson discusses as compulsive anti-essentialism or anti-essentialist essentialism (Wilson 1998). I have sometimes been frustrated by the failure of these groups—in both of which I gladly claim membership—to communicate with each other without underlying elements of either disdain or anxiety. There is something true in many "practice-centered" and "theory-centered" perspectives, and there is also something missing, and this missing thing is located in a more thorough investigation of the integration of these perspectives. Or perhaps it is located in the gap—the synapse?—waiting to be leapt between the two.

We all struggle as actors to figure out how best to embody the characters we play, which often requires us to engage a breathtaking expanse of desires and drives (in my case, these have included, among others, Sonia in *Uncle Vanya* and Charlotta Ivanovna in *The Cherry Orchard*, Desdemona in *Othello* and Isabella in *Measure for Measure*, Regina in *Little Foxes*, Bananas Shaughnessy in *The House of Blue Leaves*, Mrs. Winemiller in *Eccentricities of a Nightingale*, and, in the past twenty years, numerous solo performance pieces, some of them original). Those of us who direct find ourselves on an ongoing quest to find ways of excavating the richest potentials out of a script and getting the best work out of diverse groups of performers. For many of us our best work comes out of a boundless love for the studio, grounded in solid research that requires us to read in a wide range of a disciplines—a quest for facts and information that deepen and anchor the acting. That is, theories and research of one kind or another always inform our practice. The "feeling" actor–director–storyteller and the "critical" performance theorist parts of ourselves are inseparable; the social and psychological complexity of acting and the tough, subjective, all too contingent practicalities of making a performance make it inevitable that we are always integrating some kind of practice and some kind of theory.

In order to address both the actor's problem of imaginatively creating and being consistently connected to a role, and to banish false theory–practice dichotomies, I will look at how developments in cognitive neuroscience, which studies the intersections of biology and cognition, might be used in a "new generation" approach to help the actor, in Stanislavsky's words, reach "unconscious creativeness through conscious technique" (Stanislavsky 1936: 50). If we begin with the organic ground of acting—the body and brain—, we can clarify what we mean when we speak of things such as self, character, and feeling—words central to the projects of both performance and theory. Since acting grows out of our biological being, what we are learning about memory and imagination, and the way emotion, reason, and physicality are ultimately inseparable in the brain's structure and function, has significant implications for how we understand what happens when we act. All acting techniques work with the same raw material, the actor's only material—the body and consciousness.

Advances in our knowledge of how the mind works are redefining how we think about who we are and how we function as people and as actors. We have an increasing ability to manipulate our sense of who we are at the mysterious point at which mind arises out of the body, e.g., through surgery or drugs, which raises basic questions about what a "self," and hence what a character or a role or emotional authenticity, might be. Memory is now known to be an often unreliable or approximate process of neural pattern reactivation: the neural patterns that are activated to "retrieve" a memory are never precisely the same thing twice, because the brain changes at least minutely with each event. Facts such as these have major implications for how we might understand the actor's "truth" and provide opportunities for enriching our sense of the uses of imagination in rehearsal and performance. These new discoveries and perspectives provide the foundation for a more personal and liberating guide to engaging a role: we can loosen ourselves from beliefs that constrain our imagination and our ability to explore the full range of human possibility. We can free ourselves from received notions of what a feeling or an action should be like, based on prior experiences or habits of thought. We can picture more vividly how the work begins with action and imagination, and allow feeling and behavior to grow out of these to sometimes surprising effect. We can be more clear with the language we use to talk about experience and technique. This book uses the science to rethink acting terms such as imagination, action, given circumstances, feeling, and memory, and explores how they and elements of experience can be more powerfully and consistently engaged. One purpose of this book is to take the next step with the kind of work begun by Stanislavsky and major Stanislavsky-influenced acting masters, increasing our appreciation for how prescient their work was, while shedding the misapprehensions of their various methods. At bottom, I hope the book sharpens our understanding of the actor's process and provides practical techniques for applying what science has discovered.

This is a book first for actors. It uses science and theory to support practical tools for contextualizing theatre practice and engaging the actor's process. Chapter 1 provides an overview of significant twentieth-century developments in sciences that have had an impact on how we think about acting. Chapter 2 considers the twentieth-century heritage of actor training, particularly as it relates to the uses of science by Stanislavsky, Meyerhold, the major Stanislavsky-based US teachers, and others. Chapter 3 presents major perspectives and principles in cognitive neuroscience that have implications for how we think about acting, and points the way toward their application

for the actor. Chapter 4 considers some of these practical applications through case studies and exercises. The Appendix is a case
study in translation, which considers the way translation powerfully
shapes and directs the actor's work through particular usages of
language, syntax, and imagery, all of which relate to cognition and
perception.

Though this book is intended first for studio use, I hope it will
also be used in performance studies research and in classes. Its goal
is to provide not only practical tools for the actor, but also to take
us more deeply into the poetry and mystery of what it means to act
and, thus, what it means to be human. From science's perspective,
we are the evolutionary and cultural result of neural patterns and
biological processes interacting with the environment, but this does
not mean there is no mystery. We still don't know precisely how
consciousness occurs, about the precise way and moment that
awareness arises out of the body, about the moment that it becomes
possible for the body to ask, as the actor does at the first rehearsal,
"Who am I?" and "Where am I?" But, because of the science, we
know more than we ever have before, and it has significance for both
the practice and theory of acting and theatre.

Chapter 1

Acting, history, and science

What a piece of work is a man! how noble in reason! how infinite in faculties! in form and moving how express and admirable! in action how like an angel! in apprehension how like a god! the beauty of the world, the paragon of animals! And yet to me what is this quintessence of dust?

(Shakespeare, *Hamlet*, II, ii)

Moreover, and this is of primary importance, *the organic bases of the laws of nature on which our art is founded will protect you in the future from going down the wrong path.*

(Konstantin Stanislavsky 1936: 16, italics in original)

Acting and science: a starting point

All the actor has is herself. Her self. As constituted by her body, intellect, feeling, and history. The actor's process is, at its core, subjective and idiosyncratic, involving the negotiation of fleeting impulses and mysteriously rising instincts and intuitions, grounded (one hopes) in solid preparatory work with the text and staging. There are crucial areas of technical mastery in voice, movement, and text work to be addressed by the actor, but the heart of the work must be a deeply private engagement with the material. The languages of acting that have been developed over the last century reflect this idiosyncrasy and difficulty. Some approaches are effective, some are rife with mystification and a lack of specificity, and it isn't unusual for an approach to have elements of both. The problem of the subjective nature of the actor's process is compounded by the personal, poetic, and sometimes pseudo-scientific or pseudo-psychological nature of the vocabularies and techniques we use. Because of the difficulties of speaking about this subjectivity, views of acting can erroneously split body from mind and feeling, or impulse and instinct from intellect. An issue that one might initially define as vaguely psychological or affective—"this actor is emotionally blocked"—may in fact have a primarily physiological basis—"this actor needs a yoga class, a better diet, more rest, etc." —, or the reverse may be the case. I believe this problem can sometimes derive from a limited or flawed sense of how the different facets of ourselves are interconnected and in fact are inseparable from each other. While subjectivity must always be an element in the actor's process and in the languages of acting—what we do, after all, *is* an art, not a science—, it is possible to understand and engage private aspects of the actor's work in more accurate and consistent ways.

At least since Diderot's *The Paradox of the Actor,* we in the West have been trying to understand what happens when the actor is acting and to learn how to act "better" and more efficaciously. Efforts to talk about acting in a systematic and coherent way exploded in the last century. We study Stanislavsky (in all of his bastardized versions) and those who followed him in one form or another—Strasberg, Meisner, Adler, Lewis, Hagen *et al.* (again, bastardized or modified, depending on your point of view). We study Michael Chekhov and the psychological gesture. We study Brecht's Verfremdungseffekt and fixing the "not-but" of the actor. We study non-text-centered approaches, among them Meyerhold and biomechanics, Artaud, and LeCoq. We study Grotowski in an effort to achieve communion, Chaikin in an effort to achieve connectedness to impulse, and Suzuki in an effort to tap into particular kinds of power and focus. The passionate arguments amongst followers of these various approaches are sometimes productive and sometimes frustrating, often simultaneously. While these approaches have wildly divergent perspectives and goals, all of them are ultimately focused on the same thing: helping the actor to use and integrate intellect, feelings, voice, and movement more powerfully and consistently. All of these teachers and visionaries work with the same raw material and the same problem: the actor's body and consciousness. Body and consciousness—or body, mind, and feelings—is a singular thing: everything that comprises consciousness derives from our physical being. A basic truth about what it means to be human is that there is no consciousness without a body. This is also a basic truth for acting: the body and the consciousness that rises out of it are the core materials of the actor's work.

Current research in cognitive neuroscience provides new insights into how the structures and processes of the brain, which is a part of the body, are related to consciousness, carrying with it the potential to deepen our understanding of acting methods. It in fact confirms some basic principles of acting's twentieth-century visionaries and master teachers; I would argue this is particularly true for Stanislavsky and his heirs. There have been major advances in understanding brain structure, processes, and consciousness that are relatively recent, occurring largely in the last quarter-century. These have radically altered earlier, long-held views of the inter-relationship of mind and body, particularly, to cite neuroscientist Joseph LeDoux, as they relate "perception, attention, memory, and thinking to underlying mechanisms in the brain" (LeDoux 2002: 23). Definitions of personhood, reason, and emotion are being rethought in light of new information about brain structure and neurochemical processes, and how these manifest in consciousness and behavior. We are also increasingly able to manipulate these through surgery and by using medications; e.g., the most significant and familiar categories of these today include selective serotonin reuptake inhibitors, or SSRIs, the group that includes Prozac and other common antidepressants; levothyroxines, that treat thyroid deficiencies; and hormone replacement therapies, all of which we use to adjust our basic sense of well being, and thereby our sense of self, by modulating chemical and hormonal balances in our body. The increasing ability to manipulate consciousness and our sense of who we are at the point at which mind arises out of the body raises a cluster of questions about what the self is, since the self—held by many to be something essential and relatively unchanging—is increasingly shown to be a manifestation of neural processes and "narrative creation" that can be significantly changed by surgical intervention to control physiological malfunction or by taking drugs to alter neurochemical processes. Aldous Huxley could barely have foreseen current developments in pharmacology and conscious-ness as he was writing *Brave New World* in 1932 or *The Doors of Perception* in 1954.

Recent advances that provide new pictures and new vocabularies for visualizing ourselves—our "selfs"—have the potential to provide actors with a more precise and personalized guide to engaging the challenges of a role. For almost a century many of us have held as an axiom of Stanislavsky-based approaches to acting, i.e., those focusing on the actor's engagement with character and story, and conveying a sense of something significant being lived in the present moment in front of an audience, are effective because they grow out of how we work emotionally and intellectually. This is because, among other things, they help us to perceive ourselves as "a self" in relationship to a particular environment and circumstances, and to construct personalized narratives about those relationships. Cognitive neuroscience takes this one step further by exploring more precisely how emotional and intellectual life grows out of our biology. The science is not limited in its application, for it can be used to approach the embodiment of characters in a range of styles and modes including, but extending beyond, psychological realism; this is in the tradition of Stanislavsky, who applied his systems not just to Chekhov and Gorky, but to Shakespeare, Molière, and Mozart. An "acting-targeted" knowledge of how the mind works provides a more concrete vocabulary and set of tools for the actor to use in rehearsal and performance. It also has the potential to feel less "loaded" in personal terms, because its ground is the general process by which all human beings work; among other things, since it doesn't spotlight the actor's individual "psyche" or "emotional sensitivity" in isolation, it can provide multiple perspectives on and ways in to acting.

As this project integrates science, acting, and postmodern performance theory, it is not without its complications and the potential for being challenged. These three fields historically have not only resistances, but also antipathies toward each other, even though theatre and performance research models generally follow paradigms of science and culture, and a number of scholars have considered how scientific and technological shifts have affected our understanding of theatre and performance. For example, Philip Auslander addresses the impact of electronic media on our understanding of liveness and authenticity in *Liveness*, and Jon McKenzie examines the impact of new technologies in a range of fields in *Perform or Else*. Most pertinent here is Joseph Roach's invaluable *The Player's Passion: Studies in the Science of Acting*, which traces the effect of changing scientific paradigms on how we have understood the actor's process; he takes us from the time of the Roman Quintilian to the mid-twentieth century, through mechanist, vitalist, biological, and psychological perspectives ranging from the behavioral to the psychoanalytic, each of which held currency in its own time, but which was superseded by the next wave of research. Interestingly, by the time Roach's work was published, first in 1985 and then in 1993, research was underway in the cognitive and neurosciences that was calling into question basic aspects of consciousness, cognition, and brain function that were going to require us to once again redefine our sense of the actor's process. Nonetheless, science, acting, and performance theory at times reject fundamental premises of the other two. The problems are similar to those of psychology—a foundational discipline for acting—in which biology and culture intersect. Some postmodern theories see science as being reductive and essentialist, and traditional acting as anti-intellectual and uncomfortably messy in terms of feelings and the body. From these postmodern perspectives, both science and acting lack sufficient cultural contextualization and therefore require rigorous interrogation; interrogation is necessary, but its terms need to be grounded in research. Science can have the same aversion to art's emphasis on "feeling" rather than reason and evidence, while finding postmodernism disconnected from fact, research, materiality, and utility. Performing arts practitioners can define their focus as experiential and emotional, rather than factual or critical, and resist being analytical or technical. We artists might see the core of our work as being antithetical to theory, failing to acknowledge that theory—an idea about how a thing works or what it means, based on observation or experience—permeates any culture-making activity. Stanislavsky-based actors might resist the application of science when it comes to understanding the subjective components of our work for fear of being too much "in our head" (as if it were possible to function without a head—but more about this later) and killing our inspiration, but this overlooks the fact that Stanislavsky, Meyerhold, and others had explicitly scientific components in their approaches to actor training.

Some of the difficulties of working in an integrated way with acting, performance theory, and science grow out of common and mistaken artificial binaries such as science vs. art, thinking vs. feeling, and reason vs. emotion. The roots of mind–body dualism go back to Plato, and these constructs became particularly significant for modern Western acting with seventeenth- and eighteenth-century philosophies, especially that of Descartes, that split mind from matter and reason from feeling. There are also other disciplinarily-related anxieties that trouble an integrated engagement with science, art, and theory. These possibly include a particular kind of anti-science bias, or what Elizabeth Wilson calls the "anti-essentialist essentialism," of some postmodern theories that reject science because it must de facto be insufficiently socially theorized and uncritically dependent on uncontextualized material observation— a reverse of some scientists' critiques of other disciplines that concentrate on the theoretical or abstract in contradiction to material evidence (Wilson 1998: 15–18). There are anxieties about loss of authority, loss of status, insecurities about realizing that we don't know what we thought we knew, concerns that our interpretations of given events or situations might need to be rethought, sometimes radically, based on new information. Perhaps a major anxiety has to do with the challenges that brain and cognitive sciences present to definitions of identity and self; these are perhaps based on the gross misunderstanding that the science is inevitably leading us to an increasingly hypermaterialistic, overdetermined definition of the human, i.e., there will eventually be not only an explanation, but a formula, to explain and ultimately control our every feeling, thought, and action, taking away our individuality and freedom, because we are no more than physiological and electrochemical processes. The fear is that the science will take away the part of us that has choice, that makes art, that makes democracy possible. This is possibly the point at which anxieties about the end of theatre—and maybe even humanity, for want of a better way of putting it—arise. Interestingly, I am convinced the reverse is true. The science, through discovering more about material functions that support consciousness, increasingly confirms the complexity and *contingency* of emotional, cognitive, and behavioral processes; these can vary considerably based upon the specific individual and her situation. The science does not take away "the human," and, hence, theatre and performance; rather, it provides tools to engage these more closely. Scientists disagree about their work at least as intensely as we do about ours; as in our fields, there is research, there is argument, there is more research, there is more argument, and things change. I could also argue that the speed of substantial change in the cognitive neurosciences easily outpaces that in our fields, which makes it challenging for individuals within those disciplines to stay current, and even more challenging for those of us using the findings of those disciplines. Further, both science and performance theory can be abused, e.g., by politicians who distort the findings of scientific research for political ends or who use the tools of rhetoric and performance to manipulate the citizenry; however, this denies neither the uses of science and performance theory, nor the fact that performance and scientific memes, paradigms, and hard and soft knowledge inform, frame, and sometimes limit how we think. The older fragmented and compartmentalized perspectives are increasingly being replaced, even in the mainstream, by ones that acknowledge the dynamic interplay among biology, environment—which, of course, includes culture—, and psychological phenomena.

We work freely and enthusiastically with the body when it comes to issues related to the actor's basic health and to vocal and movement training. All reputable training programs follow the principle that the more we know about things such as the vocal mechanism, kinesiology, careful practice in stage combat, diet, hydration, conditioning, and rest, the better off we are as performers and the more skillful and safe we can be in our work. But some are reluctant to deal with intellectual and feeling aspects of the actor's work with the same kind of technical rigor. However, just as good vocal and physical technique—good bio-science, if you will—liberates us as actors, so too can a more accurate technique for other aspects of the actor's craft. Though there is a material ground—the brain—for memory, feeling, and imagery, and for our sense of authenticity, our understanding of these more subjective or interpretive aspects of our craft can tend to stop at impressions or received theories. Some of this no doubt has to do with our Cartesian and Freudian heritages. But another major factor is that until recently we simply haven't known enough to proceed further; the neuroscience has only in recent decades reached the stage at which we can begin to look at these things in a materially meaningful way. We are finally beginning to know enough about how the thing that gives rise to impressions and theories—the brain itself, in the body—works.

"Who am I?" and "Where am I?" are not only questions we ask ourselves every day in one way or another, as people and as actors, but they are also the basic ongoing concerns of any organism, which is always asking itself these questions, both consciously and unconsciously, as it negotiates its environment. These are the questions by which the organism tries to address its state of being, in order better to survive. So, in an effort to locate ourselves historically and culturally—to address for the actor a "Where am I?" of our particular moment—, what follows is a brief overview of some major developments in science and culture in the last century and a half. Its purpose is to provide a ground for considering issues addressed in later chapters.

History: a contemporary context

We have been moving at an ever-quickening pace in the last 150 years. Increasingly rapid changes in technologies and knowledge are the order of the day. It has been a century and a half since Charles Darwin's publication of *On the Origin of the Species* in 1859 fundamentally changed our sense of biology and what it means to be human (indeed, the term "biology" itself first appeared only in 1801–1802 in the writings of Lamarck and Treviranus). At roughly the same time, we entered new phases in the fields of neurology and psychology. It could be argued that the ground for modern neurology was laid in 1861 when French physician Pierre-Paul Broca presented the first of his major reports that began to link aspects of cognition to specific parts of the brain, through his description of how damage in particular areas was connected to impaired speech; a further step was taken in 1874 when German physician Carl Wernicke described the linkage of the inability to comprehend speech to another part of the brain. Another crucial step in the development of psychology as a modern discipline was the founding of the first experimental psychology laboratory by Wilhelm Wundt in the late 1870s, marking a definitive splitting off of psychology from philosophy; until that time the disciplines had been relatively indivisible, though today it would not occur to most of us to think of philosophy and psychology as the same field. In 1900, Freud, having left behind his own work in research psychology to embrace psychoanalysis, published *The Interpretation of Dreams*, and within a few decades his language of the subconscious became the dominant currency in the US for thinking about human behavior and emotional life; though difficult to imagine, prior to Freud it would not have been possible to consider the subconscious or drives in ways that many have since assumed to be an accurate way to view our inner lives. In the same year, Max Planck formulated quantum theory, and five years later Einstein published the special theory of relativity. Both of these forced a rethinking of the universe in the most subatomic and universal ways that now seem commonplace: of course, we now know, an event can be a particle or a wave, depending on how it is measured; of course, time and space are relative; of course, the observer is not separate from the event being observed, but is part of the event. These facts permeate our understanding and have been central to some of the most significant innovations in theatre, particularly in the last three decades, in both technology and in dramatic literature. Another significant event in psychology occurred in 1906, when the Russian Ivan Pavlov published his findings about reflex responses, setting the course for behavioral approaches to psychology that would rival Freud's psychoanalytic one; this was the same year that Stanislavsky first began his experiments in analyzing and systematizing the actor's process. In short, at the turn of the last century our basic sense of body, mind, feeling, time, and space was being revolutionized.

The developments of the early twentieth century laid the groundwork that would eventually give rise to cognitive science in the latter half of the 1950s, when a number of disciplines—primarily psychology, linguistics, and computer science—were brought together in a new way. Over the first half of the century psychology encompassed multiple movements. Basic facts of human nature were contested; views ranged from Freud's emphasis on the unconscious to the James-Lange theory that behavior precedes feeling (a significant influence on Meyerhold's biomechanics) to Skinner's strict behaviorism of the early 1950s that asserted that all we are is materially and behaviorally conditioned, and there is no unconscious, no soul. Linguistics was formally founded as a discipline in the first decade of the century by, among others, Ferdinand de Saussure, the father of semiotics (see, for example, his *Course in General Linguistics*, 1916). Meanwhile, beginning in 1914, Russian literary critics, most prominently Viktor Shklovsky, developed a relatively technical approach to the study of poetic language that became known as formalism. These laid the ground for structuralism, a term coined in 1929 by Russian linguist Roman Jakobson, who drew on both of these arenas. All of this, among other influences, eventually underpinned the thinking of Noam Chomsky, who, opposing Skinner's behaviorism, argued for innate "language structures" in the brain.

During these same decades computer science became a significant field. Initial developments in what would become digital technology occurred. The first freely programmable computer was invented in 1936 (by way of context for the actor, this was the year in which *An Actor Prepares* was published); transistors were invented in 1948, the first sophisticated computer language (Fortran) in 1954, and computer chips in 1958 (again, for context, this is three years before the posthumous publication of *Creating a Role* in 1961); all of these led to significant advances in the sophistication and speed with which computers processed their data. The speed of data processing allowed by chips and new computer codes were among the developments that led computer scientists to think about the nature and processes of their machines in relationship to the processes of the human brain.

In the latter half of the 1950s, a group of psychologists, computer scientists interested in artificial intelligence, and linguists—most prominently, Chomsky—founded the field of cognitive science in order to study the acquisition and processing of knowledge in a multifaceted way; among its goals was to counter the reductive materialism of Skinner's behaviorism and his principle of operant conditioning that virtually denied the existence of "mind." This new approach to understanding and manipulating the storage and operations of information would provide new ways of thinking about—and new metaphors for—how we think.

Meanwhile in theatre, during these same decades there was a revolution in actor training in the US. By the 1930s Stanislavsky was drawing on his experience in the theatre and on the science of the experimental psychologists Théodule Ribot, William James, and Carl Lange, among others, in order to write *The Actor Works on Himself (Rabota aktera nad soboi,* published in two parts in the Soviet Union*),* the first part of which appeared in English in 1936 as *An Actor Prepares.* Coming out of a shared Stanislavsky-influenced experience of the American Laboratory Theatre and the Group Theatre, by the 1950s and 1960s Lee Strasberg, Stella Adler, and Sanford Meisner had moved to the center of US actor training, establishing their approaches to acting by appropriating elements of Stanislavsky and incorporating their own theories of human psychology and behavior, some of them directly drawn from Pavlov and Freud, among others. These approaches have dominated text-centered actor training in the US ever since. Outside of the US there have, of course, been important physically based or non-"psychologically" based approaches to actor training, such as those of Jerzy Grotowski and Tadashi Suzuki, but none of these has had the pervasive effect that Stanislavsky and his heirs have had on the US view of what acting is and how it should be taught. However, while text-centered actor training in the US has tended to remain grounded in mid-twentieth century versions of Stanislavsky-derived approaches, the science on which these approaches were premised has continued to move ahead.

Though first-generation cognitive science (that of roughly the 1950s to the 1980s) was valuable for the insights it provided into our processes of cognition and response, it did not cover all aspects of its subject, tending to marginalize or omit some material aspects of the body, including some of the ways in which the brain actually works. The physical source of cognition was being studied in another field as, from the 1930s to the 1960s, neuroscientists were making new forays into examining brain structure and function. Focusing on the "wetware" of the brain (as opposed to the "software" provided by experience and learning), they, among other things, identified more locations in the brain for select functions; discovered the chemical nature of synaptic transmission; learned how, in some cases, brain anatomy could be altered by experience; and defined some mechanics of memory function (for example, that protein plays a role in memory formation). The neuroscientists were developing a material understanding of how the brain—and hence the mind—works.

Discoveries and developments in neuroscience, technology, and genetics are requiring us to move beyond perspectives that limit themselves to Freud's psychoanalysis, Skinner's behaviorism, and even the computer-inspired models of some earlier forms of cognitive science. By 1970 it was proven that synaptic changes in the brain could be related to memory and its "storage," i.e., a memory was a measurable, physical event, marked by an alteration in neural structure. By the end of the seventies, positron emission tomography (PET scans) made it possible actually to begin to see the brain at work; following the injection of radioactive isotopes into a person's brain, the person is placed in a scanner that produces a series of slice images to create a picture of the brain's anatomy. In 1990, the invention of functional magnetic resonance imagery (fMRI) expanded our ability by providing images of dynamic processes, i.e., we could see the brain at work by measuring neural activity related to changes in blood oxygen levels. We now have the ability to take pictures of, among other things, some processes of perception, attention, emotion, memory, and sensation. Discoveries in genetics are working in conjunction with neuroscience to provide even more insight into the roots of consciousness and behavior. In the same year as fMRI, gene knockout technology was invented, radically advancing the possibilities for medical science; this ability to remove or alter genes or gene sequences began to allow us to connect physical and behavioral characteristics to specific genes or combinations of genes. (A caveat: though it is tempting to think about this in reductive terms, e.g., as a direct one-to-one correlation between gene and trait, the correlations are not so simple, and environmental factors greatly affect the development of genetic predisposition.) The first significant application of this technology to neuroscience occurred in 1993, when it helped lead to the discovery of the gene responsible for Huntington's disease, a disease of not just physical, but also intellectual and emotional deterioration. This was a significant step in uncovering the links among genetic make-up, brain function, and the most basic aspects of a person's conscious life. A line could now be drawn from the gene to the brain to the mind—the "self." Actors often speak of feeling "connected" or "disconnected"; the science is giving us vivid pictures of just how our connections work.

Pharmacology has also raised significant issues. Drugs are increasingly powerful in their ability to alter our sense of our self by altering our neurochemical balance. Many psychopharmaceuticals work by mimicking, or even literally reproducing, some naturally occurring neurotransmitters (chemicals that carry messages between different nerve cells or between nerve cells and muscle cells to trigger or prevent an impulse) and repressing others, sometimes changing not just our emotional state, but also our basic sense of being. We have come a long way since the introduction of Ritalin in 1950 and Thorazine in 1952. Mood-altering drugs such as Prozac, a selective serotonin reuptake inhibitor invented in 1987 designed to regulate serotonin, a key neurotransmitter, now seem as common as aspirin used to be. By changing our brains, these drugs change our thoughts and feelings.

Another field that has had an impact on how we view and construct ourselves is cybertechnology, which has fundamentally shifted our sense of our place in the world through redefining our relationship to time and space. Some key events in the progress of this discipline include: the invention of the Ethernet in 1973; the appearance of consumer computers in 1974 (the Apple I was introduced in 1976); the testing of cellular phones in 1979; the term "cyberspace" was coined by William Gibson in 1984; in 1990 Tim Berners-Lee of MIT wrote the prototype for the world wide web, using URLs, HTML, and HTTP. A fascinating development occurred in 1991, when the Japanese government made plans to develop a sixth-generation computer based on—of all things —neural networks: computer scientists were now modeling computers based on neurology, in a reverse of the earlier cognitive scientists who modeled theories of the brain on how computers worked. Cybertechnology also increasingly interfaces with the body, blurring the line between what is human and what is computer. For the last twenty years, feminist theorist and cyber-philosopher Donna Haraway has written extensively and provocatively about how the new technologies have permeated and altered our consciousnesses (for those of you who are *Star Trek* fans, she has even argued that we are all now borg). In 1998, Kevin Warwick, a professor of cybernetics at the University of Reading, conducted a range of exercises. One included implanting a chip in his arm to track his movement, thereby allowing lights and appliances to be turned on as he arrived in a given room of his house and turned off as he left. Soon after, while visiting Columbia University in New York, he transmitted his neural signals via the Internet to move a robotic hand in the UK. In this situation, where exactly is "Kevin Warwick"?

Who are we, if we are not our thoughts and feelings? Even more revolutionary questions about the boundaries and nature of the self are being raised by research on mirror neurons. This field promises to shift radically our sense of what it means to be in relationship to another, and what it means to be autonomous and to have certain kinds of freedom in our responses. In 1996, Giacomo Rizzolatti and his colleagues at the University of Parma, who had been conducting experiments with monkeys, published their findings that the monkeys' brains contain a special class of cells:

> neurons that respond to a particular kind of gesture, no matter who is making the gesture—the monkey whose brain activity is being recorded, or another monkey. If the monkey being recorded reaches for a grape, areas in the animal's prefrontal lobes discharge. If another monkey, or even a human, reaches for the grape, the neurons of the monkey observing the action also discharge. In short, the neurons mirror both activities of the self and activities of others directed at the same goal.
>
> (Gazzaniga 2005: 104)

From the perspective of mirror neurons, sometimes called "monkey see, monkey do" neurons, watching something is the same as doing something—the same neuron fires. Some researchers now argue that human brains have "multiple mirror neuron systems that specialize in carrying out and understanding not just the actions of others, but their intentions, the social meaning of their behavior and their emotions" (Blakeslee 2006). This same article quotes

Rizzolatti: "Mirror neurons allow us to grasp the minds of others not through conceptual reasoning but through direct simulation. By feeling, not by thinking." To be sure, there is disagreement about the precise function of mirror neurons in relationship to non-motor functions, but this is spurring on intensive ongoing research into not only mirror neurons, but also other types of neurons connected to simulation that let us connect to other people in terms of both action and empathy, and that make it possible for us to imitate each other. The general implications of this research are profound. Language and culture would not exist without imitation; we learn by looking and copying, e.g., an infant will copy a parent sticking out a tongue or making noises or clapping hands as she develops. Some scientists now posit that imitation would not exist without mirror neurons. The specific implications of these discoveries for actors are considerable, for mirroring and simulation types of neurons may be at the heart of some aspects of creativity, particularly in terms of imitation and possibly empathy. The nature of the arguments between Plato and Aristotle regarding the power of imitation and of watching gain fresh strength, and Diderot's eighteenth-century discussion of the actor's paradox and the superiority of the actor without feeling requires reconsideration. Further, these findings finally and definitively set aside the tired acting binary of "inside-out" vs. "outside-in." Some of the most profound questions raised by these discoveries have to do with the relationship between ourselves and others, for what does it mean if my mind is activated identically to yours when you move your hand? What in fact are the boundaries between your feelings and mine, your actions and mine?

allocentric

So who is it that is doing the acting? We value presence, honesty, and authenticity in acting, but what is the thing that is present or authentic? What are our habits of thought, our habits of feeling in assessing these essential but intangible qualities? If we are acting, what do we feel or think we feel in this state (and I daresay all of us who act have had performances that we thought were wretched and that audiences loved and vice versa)? If we are in the audience, we can ask the same questions. As developments in science and technology almost daily demand that we alter our relationship to our inner and outer worlds in new, sometimes challenging, sometimes exciting ways, these questions become increasingly complex and fascinating. Lines blur between the human and the technological, as implants in the brain are used to affect electrical function, and between the human and the chemical, as we use new drugs to shape how we feel about ourselves and our place in the world. We are learning more and more about the physical, electrical, and chemical grounds out of which our intellectual and emotional lives arise—and hence about the matter and material of the actor and her work.

Cognitive science is a general umbrella term that encompasses cognitive psychology, neuroscience, neurolinguistics, and cognitive anthropology, among other specializations, and there is a wide array of neurocognitive models that can inform an assessment of what it is that we do when we act. What follows is an overview of a few that can provide a beginning framework for how to think about applying the science to acting. All of the models I discuss address basic categories of unified theories of cognition and adhere to the premise that consciousness—which includes intellectual thought and feeling—is a manifestation of the body, and that the parts of ourselves are not split or separate from each other. The scientists I cite begin with hard data and careful research in order to construct theories with varying degrees of speculation, and which are contested to varying degrees within their disciplines. In spite of the speculation and contestation—perhaps even because of this in some instances—, each of them has something to offer toward a deeper way of thinking about acting and which might open some fruitful speculation. These theories can be seen as falling under two large disciplinary umbrellas: models that are based in cognitive psychology and cognitive linguistics, and models based in neuroscience. There is significant overlap among these, but, for the purposes of the brief survey that follows, I am dividing the descriptions very roughly, and even reductively, between models that focus on cognition and language, and those that focus on the relationship of cognition to the way the brain works.

Cognitive psychology and cognitive linguistics

Among the cognitive psychology and cognitive linguistic models that can inform thinking about acting are the theatre of consciousness/global workspace theory of Bernard Baars; George Lakoff and Mark Johnson's theory of the body as the source of dominant metaphors that shape consciousness; Gilles Fauconnier and Mark Turner's theory of conceptual blending; and computational theories of mind, as described by Steven Pinker and Daniel Dennett, among others.

Global workspace theory

Psychologist Bernard Baars uses neuroscience to theorize that consciousness occurs in a central "workspace" in the brain that is supported by a massive number of non-conscious processes distributed throughout the brain. The workspace theory informs the work of many cognitive scientists, but I use Baars as the exemplar because he specifically describes this theory in terms of a "theatre of consciousness," a site of consciousness supported by a deep and broad range of unconscious activities, much like the performance on a stage is supported by a huge amount of backstage, front-of-house, and directorial work. Baars argues that our minds basically hold the matter at hand at center stage, in the spotlight of attention, while myriad unconscious "backstage" activities operate to support our conscious activity (Baars 1997). This theatrical model is metaphorical, for there is no particular, single site of consciousness in the brain, but it allows us to visualize the processes of consciousness. Like the other theories described here, this one holds that consciousness is a crucial biological adaptation; it has a great array of functions that both affects and is affected by unconscious activities and functions. Interestingly, Baars asserts that all unified theories of cognition are theatre models, with onstage and offstage functions, which might be roughly correlated with conscious and unconscious functions. (This also reflects our culture's general fascination with using theatre and performance as metaphors for many experiences and situations.)

The body as the source of metaphor and meaning

In *Philosophy in the Flesh: The Embodied Mind and Its Challenge to Western Thought*, linguist George Lakoff and philosopher Mark Johnson draw heavily on three major findings of cognitive science to develop an argument that our sense of our bodies, indeed, the fact of having a body, is the source for our major metaphors of thought, meaning, and values: first, the mind is inherently embodied; second, thought is largely unconscious; and, third, abstract concepts are largely metaphorical. In their view, reason is shaped by these: "the body; a cognitive unconscious to which we have no direct access; and metaphorical thought of which we are largely unaware" (Lakoff and Johnson 1999: 7). They hold that fundamental metaphors of time (such as "time is money," "time was rushing by"), space ("she felt distant"), events and causation ("I was walking on eggshells"), selfhood ("I just let myself go"), and morality ("he had no backbone") that pervade our thinking and speech, and that are the principal tools by which we construct meaning, grow directly out of our sense of our *physical* being: "An embodied concept is a neural structure that is actually part of, or makes use of, the sensorimotor system in our brains. *Much of conceptual inference is, therefore, sensorimotor inference*" (Lakoff and Johnson 1999: 20, italics added). That is, a concept is a particular state in the brain—and, hence, de facto a physical state. A crucial implication of this is that the metaphors we live by (to use the title of one of their books) are not just abstract or poetic, but are of our bodies in the most immediate way. Based on what we are learning about cognition and language, their argument provides a holistic way of understanding ourselves and the way language arises directly out of our physical beings: consciousness, reason, and language are a direct manifestation of our bodies and the sense we have of ourselves as bodies. One of the key implications of this is that actors do not need to "make up" or construct a way of mending the splits in themselves; they need to develop a more accurate picture of themselves as being already necessarily integrated.

Conceptual blending

Cognitive scientists and linguists Gilles Fauconnier and Mark Turner hold perspectives similar to those of Lakoff and Johnson, particularly in the prominence they give to metaphor in their theory. Their network model of conceptual integration begins to account for the way we put together associations from widely divergent situations and experiences. In *The Way We Think: Conceptual Blending and the Mind's Hidden Complexities*, they begin with two key assertions: first, imagination is the central engine of meaning and, second, metaphor is central to cognition (Fauconnier and Turner 2002). These assertions about the primacy of imagination and metaphor are particularly pertinent for acting. In this model, different mental spaces—small conceptual packets, or images, constructed as we think and talk—are integrated in novel ways to help us negotiate our lives. Disparate "inputs" are blended to create new knowledge, insight, or experience that goes beyond that contained in the initial inputs, i.e., to create a blended conceptual space. To use one of their examples, one might think of the image of a waiter carrying a tray as an aid in learning to ski down a hill more effectively; intuitively, this combination makes sense to us, though the two inputs are in fact very different movement problems. Nonetheless, we are somehow able to blend the inputs kinesthetically to accomplish the task of skiing. Though conceptual blending is consciously cognitive on one level—we are able to describe or depict it—, it primarily operates unconsciously; precisely how we do the blending is largely not in our awareness. Blending is not the same thing as making an analogy, a less complex process in which there is typically an obvious one-to-one correlation between things; in blending, significant, unconscious acts of translation and, especially, transformation must occur for the things being blended, e.g., tray-carrying and skiing, to fit together. Blending organizes and processes huge amounts of conceptual meaning to result finally in something that our conscious awareness can grasp on one level, but that also affects us in ways about which we're unaware. When we use the image of the waiter to help us ski, there is a huge amount going on automatically and unconsciously in our bodies beyond the level of mere analogy.

Computational theories of mind

Some cognitive scientists such as Daniel Dennett and Stephen Pinker, who is also a linguist, posit that the brain—and hence the mind—is like a computer. Using models that seem to me more analogical than blended, and hence less nuanced and accurate, they assert that the neuronal pathways of the brain are similar to a computer's circuitry. Pinker's model, described in *How the Mind Works*, asserts that all things mental, including beliefs and desires, are information converted into symbols that are "physical states of bits of matter, like chips in a computer or neurons in the brain" (Pinker 1997: 25). Some of these models, including Pinker's and Dennett's, are hypermaterialist, positing that all phenomena, including consciousness, are solely the manifestation of the workings of matter; in this regard, they have some similarities to hypermaterialist behavioral models, but they are quite different in that they reject theories related to operant conditioning. Computational models can be a useful way to begin to relate the science to acting, since, at their basic level, they provide an accessible, simple schematic that makes it possible to see parallels between basic terms of cognitive neuroscience and those used in actor training. This was in fact where I began my research. However, relatively quickly I grew to believe that, though these theories provided an entry point, they failed to account sufficiently for the complexity of human response and of our biological processes.

What all of these cognitive psychology models have in common is that they define some kind of *imagination*—in the sense of consciously and unconsciously imaging certain problems and situations —as a foundation for our functioning in all regards. The study of where and how these images rise to consciousness out of the matter of our brain and being is the provenance of neuroscience.

Neuroscience

We do not yet know all of the steps by which "matter becomes imagination" (to use a phrase from Gerald Edelman and Giulio Tononi). However, how elements of consciousness and behavior relate to brain function is becoming increasingly clear, getting us closer to the time when we might have a more complete answer to the question of how consciousness arises out of the brain. Some scientists who are informative on this point are Elizabeth Wilson, Joseph LeDoux, and Edelman and Tononi, who focus in different ways on the neural substrate of consciousness; and, particularly, the somatic marker hypothesis of Antonio Damasio.

The synaptic self

Some neuroscientists theorize that who we are and how we function are based largely upon potentials for specific neural patterns—or synaptic connections—in the brain and how they develop. In *Neural Geographies: Feminism and the Microstructure of Cognition*, Elizabeth Wilson describes how connectionist models

> figure cognitive processing as the spread of activation across a network of interconnected, neuron-like units [. . .] It is the connections between these units, rather than the units per se, that take on the pivotal role in the functioning of the network.
> (Wilson 1998: 6)

This is significant for it means that "Knowledge is implicit, stored in the connections rather than the units," in the paths from neuron to neuron (Wilson 1998: 160). Meaning arises from "the spatial arrangement of the connectionist architecture and the temporal vicissitudes of the activation rules," i.e., how the potentials for the brain's connections are affected in the moment of being activated (Wilson 1998: 162). Joseph LeDoux has written extensively on brain networking and cellular aspects of brain function, most notably in *Synaptic Self: How Our Brains Become Who We Are* and *The Emotional Brain*. Though we do not consciously operate on this level as actors or in our daily lives, the perspective illuminates how we— most fundamentally, in our sense of our self—are in fact a product of the workings of our synapses, the gaps between our neurons that are bridged by chemicals or an electrical impulse that allow us to function in all regards. This is not a reductive model: LeDoux discusses extensively how nature (our genetic make-up) and nurture (our experiences) are merely different ways of doing the same thing—wiring synapses in the brain, so that the connections in our brains are the result of complex, dynamic interactions between these two aspects of ourselves, that in fact are constantly changing the brain. These synaptic patterns, the potential with which we are born and which are shaped by the experiences we have, are the material ground of our conscious awareness and unconscious responses; as such, they are the product of both evolutionary and personal development. Since every experience our brain records changes our synapses, the way our synapses are "wired" is the result of learning of all kinds—cognitive, sensory, and kinesthetic (LeDoux 2002: 68). Because the brain has a high degree of plasticity, neural nets are changed and the actual size of cortices (parts of the brain) can even increase with stimulation, e.g., the sizes of string musicians' cortices devoted to their hands are significantly larger than cortices of non-musicians. In this view, memory can be seen as a kind of learning, for a memory is neurophysiologically the construction and reactivation of dynamic neural patterns. One of the most significant insights of this work is that it allows us to view learning and memory not as mental "contents" of experience per se, connected to a particular neuron or two, but as the product of synaptic patterns activated and reactivated to carry those meanings. It is the activation of these neural patterns that allows us to retrieve the "content" of the memory, to function, to make choices. From LeDoux's perspective, we are our synaptic patterns—the chemical and electrical connections made from neuron to neuron—the connections made selectively among billions of gaps. We are created in the space between. This dynamic view will be discussed in some detail later, because it has major implications for the actor's relationship to, understanding of, and use of her basic tools, particularly memory and imagination.

The neural substrate of consciousness

Neurobiologist Gerald Edelman and psychiatrist Giulio Tononi, in *A Universe of Consciousness: How Matter Becomes Imagination*, among other sources, attempt to unravel how brain gives rise to mind. While the answer to this problem is incomplete, they provide a perspective that might move us closer to solving this mystery. Edelman and Tononi believe that higher brain functions, including consciousness, are conditioned by and require interactions with the world and other people, i.e., mind is a result of what is outside of us, as well as what is inside of us. Like LeDoux, they posit that consciousness arises from specific neural processes, but they discuss more fully some implications of the interactions of brain and body with environment. They work with three assumptions: the physics assumption, which holds that only physical processes are needed to explain consciousness, i.e., mind arises from the brain, so no mind–body dualism is necessary (or allowed); the evolutionary assumption, which states that consciousness evolved during natural selection and is generated by a certain morphology, i.e., consciousness arose only because of a very specific evolution of the physical body, including the brain; and the qualia assumption, which states that the subjective—or qualitative or personal—aspects of consciousness cannot be communicated fully or "translated" directly by science, because consciousness is a private, subjective experience and science is public and intersubjective (Edelman and Tononi 2000). The problem of qualia is an elemental part of why talking about the process and experience of acting is so difficult; one person can never fully know what another is feeling or perceiving.

The somatic marker hypothesis

Neuroscientist Antonio Damasio's somatic marker hypothesis explains the interconnection of reason, emotion, and body/brain. In Damasio's view, described in *The Feeling of What Happens:*

Body and Emotion in the Making of Consciousness, as well as other sources, the brain creates strings of associations arising in the body first as an emotion (a term used by Damasio and other neuro-scientists to describe a physiological state of the body), which is translated into a feeling (a "registration" of an emotional state), which then leads to behavior, which is a response to all of the preceding that may or may not be associated with reason or rational thought. This sequence is not uncomplicated, since behavior often precedes awareness and direct feeling. Damasio uses the term "somatic marker" to describe how body-states become linked with our conscious responses to or interpretations of them. This can involve the linking of fear or pleasure with a particular situation (e.g., seeing a tiger may cause a rush of adrenalin and a whole array of other neurochemical responses, which then become linked to conscious thoughts of fear or excitement or wonder; or thinking about a loved one may cause both a rush of endorphins and a shift in our respiration). These markers become our repertory of emo-tional, i.e., body-state, responses in guiding our choice of reactions to new situations. This was initially a mechanism for maximizing survival, for it reduces the range of possible choices through which we have to sort, allowing us to respond with varying degrees of habit or spontaneity, in order to be better able to save ourselves without having to think a lot about it; as with all of the workings of the brain, much of this occurs pre- or unconsciously. This hypothesis presents a way of picturing body, feeling, and intellect not as separate, but as aspects of a single organic process. Particu-larly pertinent for the actor is Damasio's assertion that reason—in the fullest sense—grows out of and is permeated by emotion, and that emotion is consistently informed by our reason and con-scious cognition. This argument is built on a meticulous study of neurophysiology—how the brain is structured and how it functions. Damasio's research and theory are a primary foundation for Chapter 3.

Where does this leave acting?

So, in light of the current science, where does this leave acting? The research seems to dislocate comfortable and familiar constructs of identity, feeling, and selfhood that have been dominant for decades. Yet we must engage the science, if we are to stay true to acting's mission of embodying aspects of human experience, and of expressing both the changing and the relatively (or seemingly) unchanging components of basic human conditions. Acting has always involved the interaction of biology and culture. As culture changes ever more rapidly and theories for discussing intersections of biology, culture, and technology evolve, most significantly in the field of performance studies, we have tried to find better and clearer ways for talking about the feelings and experiences that we have while performing or while watching a performance. Inevitably, our world-view (or paradigm or episteme, call it what you will) establishes the ground for how we understand our bodies and, hence, ourselves. It is impossible to separate views of the actor's process from the dominant scientific views of any given historical period. How we understand acting is contingent, even if only implicitly, on how we understand basic human functioning. The explicit use of science to illuminate acting has a long tradition, most fully described by Roach's *The Player's Passion*, mentioned earlier, which traces the changing major scientific and philosophical paradigms from the Greeks to the twentieth century and how they provided foundations for changing views of the actor's process. What becomes obvious through Roach's study is that, as paradigms of science change, so too do paradigms of acting. While biological evolution proceeds at a relatively slow pace (though it *does* proceed) and we are not all that different from the ancient Greeks or the Elizabethans in this regard, there have been huge and increasingly rapid changes in culture and technology. It is important to distinguish between what is (relatively) "unchanging" about acting and views of acting that are the products of particular historical moments. It is tempting, but ultimately counterproductive, to hang on to models, or even components of models, that have outlived their use.

So what has remained constant (so far) in acting? Terms that keep surfacing are the "real," the "natural," the "imitative," the "realistic," the "truthful," character, action, and emotion (or feeling), to mention a few. These are being complicated in interesting ways in our contemporary culture, as popular forms, media, and technologies keep shifting the ground of what we understand these to be. Autobiographical solo performance, "reality" television, and productions that integrate live and digitally manufactured components are among the current forms changing the present and charting a course for the future. It is impossible to predict what other forms of performance will arise in the next decade. However, among the things that connect the current forms to each other and to the theatre and theatrical forms of the past is narrative, either in the telling of or in the creating of a story. All of these forms are also built on imagination and action—motivated behavior as a response to a set of given circumstances. Cognitive neuroscience clarifies the biological ground of these human fundamentals and provides insight into the foundations of the actor's process.

This work will not completely demystify what we do when we act, but I hope it will change the sense of what and where the mystery is in the process. Because of the private nature of consciousness, a significant subjective component in acting will remain undefinable for the foreseeable future. And, as Edelman and Tononi write, "our own private consciousness is, in a profound sense, all there is." My goal here is to direct us to the deeper poetry and mystery of what it means to act and, thus, what it means to be human.

Chapter 2

The twentieth-century heritage

> "*Je pense, donc je suis.*"/ "*Cogito ergo sum.*"
>
> (René Descartes)

> "*Je suis, . . . ergo sum.*"
>
> (Moon in *The Real Inspector Hound*, Stoppard 1968: 23)

> "Mind you, only physical actions, physical truths, and physical belief in them! Nothing more!"
>
> (Stanislavsky 1936: 142)

> "Who's there?"
>
> (Shakespeare, *Hamlet* I, i, line 1)

A problem that pervades US acting today, implicitly and sometimes explicitly, is compartmentalization: mind is separated from body, feeling from intellect, reason from emotion. The misapprehension of what we are and how we operate has its roots in Plato, but for our purposes it can be traced back most importantly to the seventeenth century, when René Descartes' dualistic view of the human being triumphed over monistic ones such as Baruch Spinoza's. Descartes defined us as the union of a thinking soul and an extended, material body that interact causally with each other, i.e., mind and body are two distinct, separate things. Spinoza, on the other hand, saw us as a finite mode or manifestation of God, existing simultaneously as both thought and extension, i.e., mind and body are identical, the same substance, in short, a form of panpsychism. Since the ascendance of Cartesian dualism, dominant philosophical and cultural perspectives have given us pictures of ourselves that are often based on splitting our parts off from each other and that sometimes privilege one aspect over another in detrimental ways; some manifestations of this might be seen in scientists who find actors too "emotional" and actors who find scientists too "rational," when in fact both the best scientists and the best actors rely on intuition, instinct, and intelligence. The truth is that these parts of our selves are inseparable: without the material of the living body, there is no mind, and without feeling, there is no true reason.

Twentieth-century approaches to acting have largely been attempts to negotiate, if not integrate, the actor's material being and what might be called the more immanent aspects of our selves. Dualisms of various kinds are taught as a basic premise in various Stanislavsky-influenced acting classes ("get out of your head," "don't think, do"), even though Stanislavsky himself was an early twentieth-century version of a monist who would likely have agreed more with Spinoza than Descartes, at least in terms of the premise that mind and feeling can't be separated from body. What is constant in Stanislavsky-based approaches to acting is the emphasis on imagination and action; it is a thread running through the heart of modern actor training that begins with Stanislavsky and his quest for a consistent way to reach inspiration in performance. His experiments in how to get the different aspects of the self—intellect, feeling, instinct, body, and voice/speech—working in an integrated and reliable way are the ground out of which others have moved or against which they have reacted. While Meyerhold, Michael Chekhov, and later Brecht rejected the reliance on affective memory of the earlier phases of Stanislavsky's system (as Stanislavsky eventually did himself), they all embraced other elements of his thinking; Meyerhold drew on the same sciences as Stanislavsky in developing biomechanics and later aspects of his work with the actor; Michael Chekhov's work with imagination and psychological gesture could not have happened without his experience of working with Stanislavsky and his protégé Evgeny Vakhtangov; and Brecht was in fact a great admirer of what Stanislavsky eventually accomplished with actor training. The major US acting teachers of the middle of the last century—Stella Adler, Sanford Meisner, and Lee Strasberg—all laid claim at one point or another to using the "true" principles initially articulated by Stanislavsky—and all misunderstood aspects of his work. Artaud rejected utterly the kind of theatre in which Stanislavsky worked, with its emphasis on the theatrically effective embodiment of a text, but Artaud nonetheless had a goal that was in some ways not that different from Stanislavsky's: to have an actor who was an "athlete of the heart," who would facilitate a sense of communion. Jerzy Grotowski was intensely trained in Stanislavsky's techniques in the 1950s, prior to his founding of the Polish Laboratory Theatre; Grotowski's vision of the actor as shaman and his principle of the *via negativa* is intimately connected to Stanislavsky's belief in both the spiritual dimensions of acting and all creativity, and the stripping away of all extraneous elements in performance in favor of rigorous mental, physical, and vocal training in the service of a transcendent theatrical experience. Joseph Chaikin, in his time with the Living Theatre, the Open Theatre, and afterward, consistently rejected American Method-based approaches to acting he had encountered in the late 1950s, with their over-emphasis on a narrow kind of psychological realism and emotional narcissism; yet there are commonalities and resonances between Chaikin and Stanislavsky, in the former's work with image, impulse, and transformation and the latter's with imagination and spontaneity. Stanislavsky's interest in creating a "science" of performance is also mirrored in the technical and organism-based elements of major movement and voice–speech techniques; to name just four, the approaches of F. M. Alexander, Moishe Feldenkreis, Kristin Linklater, and Patsy Rodenburg all consider the links among body, impulse, imagination, relaxation, and concentration—terms first used in an integrated way by Stanislavsky.

What follows is a consideration of how imagination and action, which serve actors in constructing narrative and its embodiment, thread their way through some major approaches to actor training, with particular attention being paid to the intersection of technique and science.

Stanislavsky

With the help of nature—our subconscious, instinct, intuition, habits, and so forth—we evoke a series of physical actions interlaced with one another. Through them we try to understand the inner reasons that give rise to them, individual moments of experienced emotions, the logic and consistency of feelings in the given circumstances of the play. When we can discover that line, we are aware of the inner meaning of our physical actions. This awareness is not intellectual but emotional in origin, because we comprehend with our own feelings some part of the psychology of our role. Yet we cannot act this psychology itself nor its logical and consecutive feelings. Therefore we keep to the firmer and more accessible ground of physical actions and adhere rigorously to their logic and consistency. And since their pattern is inextricably bound up with that other inner pattern of feelings, we are able through them to reach the emotions. That pattern becomes part and parcel of the score of a role.

(Stanislavsky 1961: 209)

Konstantin Stanislavsky (1863–1938) has had a greater impact on American acting than any other figure. His languages of acting—and later appropriations and bastardizations of them—are ubiquitous in rehearsals, studios, and classrooms. The vocabulary of given circumstances, "if," throughline, objective, and action is common currency, and yet the system was never a singular or codified set of rules. Rather, Stanislavsky's methods were a living process of exploration and problem solving, directly connected to his path as an artist and teacher, grounded in the culture and science of his time. Since he was committed to a life in the theatre and on the stage as a process, I have no doubt that he would approve the current, ongoing explorations and dialogue about acting. (Most significantly Joseph Roach and Sharon M. Carnicke have written at length about these issues in relationship to Stanislavsky.)

Stanislavsky was fascinated by the great actors of his time, such as Duse and Chaliapin, whose "bodies were at the call and beck of the inner demands of their wills" (Stanislavsky 1948: 463). His career was driven by his desire to develop and strengthen this capacity in himself and in his actors, and early on he began to seek an approach to acting that would engage the actor consistently and vitally with the role. While his language in translation is problematic (Carnicke has an entire chapter in *Stanislavsky in Focus* on one word alone, *perezhivanie*, Stanislavsky's term typically translated as "living" or "experiencing" the part, but which is more accurately translated as "living *through*" or "experiencing *through*" the part), it is clear that Stanislavsky's aim was to develop a method that would help the actor achieve a level of consistency and excellence in performing text-based roles. Though his goal was to systematize the actor's process, he acknowledged that any system would inevitably be provisional since its value would lie in its efficacy, not in its elegance as a theory. His appetite for research and exploration was omnivorous: he experimented with the actor's process pragmatically in the studios and rehearsal; he worked in a broad range of theatrical genres (including opera); he used Raja yoga to condition the actor not just physically, but mentally through the uses of meditation and visualization; he used eurythmics to shape the actor's physical work; he used tools regarding task structure and organization he had learned from his father's manufacturing business; and he drew on scientific materialism. His reading in experimental psychology of the early twentieth century, including the writings of Théodule Ribot, among others, had a major and ongoing impact on his thinking and practice.

Stanislavsky had reached a point of crisis in his acting by 1906. He had been playing the same roles for a number of years and felt himself becoming bored and stale in them; he sensed himself to be less present in the work, particularly in the role of Dr. Stockman in *An Enemy of the People*. Craving a way to find life and immediacy again in performance, he began to organize his thinking about acting that year in a draft document, *Manual on Dramatic Art*. This was Stanislavsky's first effort to articulate a "grammar" of acting, and the seeds of his future thinking about an integrated approach to acting are here. This early grammar had two basic principles: first, the actor has to draw on all of her experiences in creating a role, and she must have a way of gaining access to these experiences on demand; second, the actor must have a way of breaking down a role into a series of units that chart the character's movement through the course of the play. Jean Benedetti posits that this "bit-by-bit" principle came from Stanislavsky's knowledge of industry (his father was a wealthy textile manufacturer) and related ways of organizing labor. Even though this technical component was significant in Stanislavsky's thinking, his goal was never anything but to find "an artistic process in tune with the processes of the human organism at the level of the un- or super-conscious," those parts of ourselves not available consciously (Benedetti 1988: 158–159). It is crucial to note that "organism" and the "unconscious" meant different things to a Russian artist in the early twentieth century than they do to an American actor in the early twenty-first. Though psychological components were central to Stanislavsky's thinking, these were not psychoanalytical in the Freudian sense, for at this time Stanislavsky wasn't familiar with Freud's work. Stanislavsky's view of the organic was based on a monistic view of the human being, i.e., mind and emotion are not separate from, but rather grow out of, the body. Rather than Freud, Stanislavsky was more influenced by the work of scientists who were experimenting with conditioned response and reflexology, a psychophysiological approach that was a precursor of early behaviorism.

By 1907 Stanislavsky was clarifying the principle of the "creative will" that he had first described the year before, which had to do with the impetus, or motivation, driving the actor. He made significant progress in this task in 1908 when he encountered the writings of experimental psychologist Théodule Ribot, specifically *Les Maladies de la Volonté* (1884), *Les Maladies de la Mémoire* (1885), and *La Psychologie des Sentiments* (1896) (translated into Russian in 1900). Ribot asserted that the will could play a positive role in a patient's recovery and that the greater the individual's desire to get better, the quicker the recovery; he also asserted that the nervous system records all memories of past experiences, and that they could be evoked by an appropriate stimulus, such as a smell or a touch (Benedetti 1988: 175). In *La Psychologie* Ribot describes the close relationship of sensory memories to memories of emotions, and specifically uses the word *sensibilité*, which can refer to both kinds of feelings—physical and affective—, in his discussion. Stanislavsky's encounter with this work led him to realize that an act of creative will could be married to the use of affective memory, i.e., the memory of a situation could be connected to a desired feeling state, as a means of connecting the actor to the character's life (Benedetti 1988: 174). By 1909 he had set out a six-stage process: stimulation of the "will" to create a commitment to the text; the use of personal material, i.e., emotion and sense memory, connected to the text; the merging of the actor's personality with the character's; physicalization, in which the actor finds the embodiment of the character; integrating these inner and the outer aspects of the character; and delivering this effectively to the audience (Benedetti 1988: 191). Stanislavsky felt the need to contextualize his research more deeply, so he began to read extensively in the history of acting, most significantly the writings of Diderot and of actors such as Clairon, Dumesnil, Talma, Luigi and Francesco Riccoboni, Ludwig Tieck, Adrienne Lecouvreur, and Coquelin. He also began exploring alternative approaches to body-mind training, incorporating eurthymics and Raja yoga into the actor's work. By 1913, through working on plays such as *Le Malade Imaginaire*, Stanislavsky was becoming increasingly convinced that character could emerge from exploring external aspects of a role and that there was no hard separation between the psychological and the physical (Benedetti 1988: 205). By 1916 he had formulated an early version of his dictum that the actor could reach the unconscious, i.e., inspiration and creativity, only through pursuing conscious objectives (Benedetti 1988: 217). One manifestation of this in his evolving approach was to shift his focus from having the actor generate a feeling that would lead to action, to having the actor define an action as the way to feeling. It is significant that Stanislavsky made this shift to what might simplistically be called an "outside-in," as opposed to "inside-out," technique early in his thinking. This seed of the method of physical action was reinforced by Stanislavsky's encounters with Ribot's discussion of the James-Lange theory of psychology as early as 1914; this theory was to have an even greater influence on Meyerhold in the 1920s.

Stanislavsky's focus on objective aspects of acting was encouraged by further developments in Russia in behavioral approaches to psychology, which held that external conditions shaped inner life and response. In the first decade of the twentieth century Ivan Sechenov wrote extensively about the reflex—the organism's reaction to external conditions—as "the essential mechanism of organic response"; in the same vein, Vladimir Bekhterëv began his research in "objective psychology" or "reflexology"; and Pavlov won the Nobel Prize for his work with conditioning in dogs (Roach 1993: 198). Though some of this research tended toward the hyper-materialist (i.e., the view that all phenomena, including thoughts and feelings, are just products of physical processes and nothing more), it was useful as an impetus for Stanislavsky for a number of reasons. Most significant among these were that it acknowledged the power of the body in relationship to mental and emotional processes, and it treated the organism as a single entity, in which physical, mental, and emotional life were all aspects of the same thing. These scientific perspectives provided something tangible with which Stanislavsky could work.

The exploration of physical and conscious aspects of performance entered an important new phase for Stanislavsky as he began research with opera singers at the Moscow Art Theatre's Music Studio in 1919. This intensive experience with singers and music at this particular phase in his explorations led him to more sophisticated thinking about tempo and rhythm. He became increasingly aware of the way that the performer's feelings and impulses were affected by a musical score's power to dictate both the speeds for each segment of the opera's action and the qualities of the singer's engagement with character. This led him to understand tempo-rhythm not as something separate from or ancillary to action, but as a crucial aspect of the action itself; in this view, by extension, attention to the tempo-rhythm of the body—a key component of the actor's physical state—became integral to the actor's feeling and psychological life. By the late 1920s Stanislavsky felt sure that finding a precise score of physical objectives, which would include attention to tempo-rhythm, was the key to the actor's success— hence, the method of physical actions. Another component of this method was precise attention to a script's language as a vital part of the physical action. In his director's notes for *Othello*, on which he worked during the late 1920s, Stanislavsky writes that for an actor to achieve the character's objectives, "he needs words, thoughts, i.e., the author's text. An actor above all must operate through words. On stage the only important thing is the active word" (*Rezhissiorsky Plan "Othello,"* Iskusstvo, 1945, qtd. in Benedetti 1988: 297). Certainly the political changes in the Soviet Union in the late 1920s, with Stalin's consolidation of power and the enforcement of a strict materialist view, would have influenced Stanislavsky in terms of the materialist components of his work, but he had been drawing on the sciences—reflexology and behaviorism—for many years already because it had provided positive results for him. And though Stanislavsky kept an eye on the political situation and in the last years of his life was under virtual house arrest, his central concern was always to help the actor engage the life of the character as vitally and passionately as possible.

In his final phase, the method of active analysis, Stanislavsky used improvisations to connect actors to physical aspects of scenes and to help them find the flow of action, using a carefully shaped "line of life of the human body" as a way to guide the "life of the human spirit." Through increasingly refined improvisations, actors would move closer and closer to the text, looking for choices that strongly connected action to text, and then reshaping the action to fit the language—an Active Analysis of the text that allowed the actor to embody the character fully by actively putting the actors' bodies into the given circumstances of a scene at the earliest stages of rehearsal. This phase is described by Carnicke and was documented most thoroughly by Stanislavsky's student, the director Maria Knebel, whose writings, sadly, are not yet available in English (Carnicke 1998).

Stanislavsky said that to play "truly" meant to be "right, logical, coherent, to think, strive, feel, and act in unison with your role" (Stanislavsky 1936: 14); in Stanislavsky's sequencing, logic, coherence, and thought precede feeling and action. He names motivated action, supported by given circumstances (which encompasses the play's narrative) and imagination (*if*), as the core of the actor's work. Stanislavsky is adamant that the actor begin with action, not feelings, since feelings arise out of something that has preceded them (Stanislavsky 1936: 41), and that the actor focus on given circumstances because they are always within conscious reach, while emotions are "of largely subconscious origin, and not subject to direct command" (Stanislavsky 1936: 51–52). The goal of the system in all of its incarnations was always the actor's success within the play as a whole, and thus it was ultimately about the actor embodying the character within the context of the play as a whole. It is evident in all of Stanislavsky's writings that the work on a character cannot be separated from the world of the play. Though some American actors using Stanislavsky (or what they think of as Stanislavsky) reject a close study of the script and assessment of how their character fits within that context, and privilege their "emotional" and private response over the "physical" or "analytical," the system consistently treats the actor and her relationship to character and text holistically. While it is possible and even necessary to focus on one aspect or another of the actor's work at a given point in the process, Stanislavsky always viewed acting as a unified, multifaceted phenomenon. "Conscious or unconscious objectives are carried out both inwardly and outwardly, by both body and soul. Therefore they can be both *physical* and *psychological*" (Stanislavsky 1961: 54). As Joseph Roach describes it:

> The Stanislavski [sic] System is a means of manipulating levels of consciousness to achieve certain specific effects on the body, especially the illusion of spontaneity. [. . .] Stanislavski [sic] believed that in life the process of adaptation is continuous. He believed that an "inner dialogue" runs within us without interruption—a stream of consciousness sustained and constantly redirected by subconscious impulses and sensory stimuli.

To both Pavlov and Stanislavski [sic], behavior consists of chains of physical adaptations, continuous transitions in the direction of the stream of consciousness caused by physical stimuli. This is the life that the actor attempts to emulate by "living the role."

(Roach 1993: 206–207)

The science was inseparable from the art for Stanislavsky. Indeed, his art grew out of science in a most basic way.

Meyerhold

Look for associative parallels! Use associative parallels in your work! So far I've only approached an understanding of the enormous power of imagery in the theatre. [. . .] You need not think that my thesis about "associations" leads to some kind of subjectivism in the perception of art. Some day physiologists, psychologists, and philosophers will show that the realm of associations is connected with certain general (and even social— after all, in the final analysis everything is social) phenomena in the majority of people.

(Meyerhold, quoted in Gladkov 1997: 163)

Lee Strasberg called Vsevolod Meyerhold (1874–1940) "the greatest director in the history of the theatre" (Gladkov 1997: 49). Stanislavsky, near the end of his life, told his production manager, Yuri Bakhrushin, "Look after Meyerhold, he is my sole heir in the theatre, not only in ours, but in the theatre as a whole" (Gladkov 1997: 43). Protégé, rival, and ultimately admirer of Stanislavsky, Meyerhold had significant differences with the older man, but both were engaged in finding ways to work with actors in invigorating and powerful ways, and both drew on elements of the scientific materialism of their time. Though Meyerhold's theatre was consistently director-centered and he never laid out a systematic method for the actor's work in the ways that Stanislavsky did, his experiments in biomechanics were an important development in the application of science to acting. And though Meyerhold eschewed affective memory and challenged Stanislavsky's approach to the actor and feeling, he firmly believed in the necessity of the actor's joy, "creative elation," and intelligence (apropos of this, he once wrote, "I have no use for actors who know how to move but cannot think" [quoted in Gladkov 1997: 104]). The most historically significant phase of Meyerhold's theorizing about acting was in the early 1920s, as he devised biomechanics, a technique for achieving maximum physical and mental preparedness and responsiveness.

Meyerhold's biomechanical exercises, initiated in 1922, were based on ideas drawn primarily from two sources that ran in parallel to aspects of Stanislavsky's thinking. The first had to do with labor. Just as Stanislavsky employed experience drawn from his family's manufacturing business to inform aspects of his system, Meyerhold drew heavily on Taylorism (a theory published by Frederick Winslow Taylor in 1911), an approach to breaking down manufacturing processes into assembly line tasks based on studies of labor efficiency; this was promoted in the new Soviet Union by Aleksei Gastev, a leading proponent of the "scientific organization of labor," with whom Meyerhold had a substantial correspondence. However, at least in this phase, Meyerhold used this science of labor for goals significantly different from Stanislavsky's, e.g., using principles of worker training, Meyerhold wanted to make the actor's use of motion as efficient as possible in accomplishing a task. The second source had to do with the psychology of the day, specifically reflexology and behaviorism. Again, the two men's differing views of the place of feeling in the actor's process led them to use the science for different ends. Meyerhold had little interest in the actor's "inner life," and he once went so far as to call the evoking of painful emotions "neurasthenic and pathological" (presaging Stanislavsky's own eventual questioning of the use of affective memory). However, the men are similar in that this research was fundamental to Meyerhold's attempts to make the actor more immediately responsive to the needs of the project. That is, both were looking for a way of making the actor more consistent and reliable in approaching any given role. Meyerhold in fact developed a relationship with Pavlov, with whom he had ongoing conversations about his efforts to develop a scientific approach to acting (Gladkov 1997: 72).

For Meyerhold, acting had two requirements:

> (1) *the innate capacity for reflex excitability,* which will enable him to cope with any emploi within the limits of his physical characteristics; (2) "physical competence," consisting of a true eye, a sense of balance, and the ability to sense at any given moment the location of his centre of gravity.
>
> (Meyerhold 1969: 199, italics in the original)

One of Meyerhold's fundamental assertions was that "All psychological states are determined by specific physiological processes" (Meyerhold 1969: 199):

> I am convinced that an actor placed in the correct physical *raccourci* [an instantaneous expressive moment, similar to a *mie* in Kabuki] will pronounce the text correctly. But after all the correct *raccourci* is also a conscious act, an act of creative thought.
>
> (Meyerhold, quoted in Gladkov 1997: 123–124)

This idea of a pattern of movement leading to a specific psychophysiological result echoes both Bekhterëv's theory of "associated motor reflexes," which asserted that human behavior is a result of the pattern of reflexes produced by the nervous system, as conditioned by habit and environment, and Stanislavsky's method of physical actions. Like Stanislavsky, Meyerhold's view of the human being was monistic, largely due no doubt to the shared scientific, cultural, and political contexts in which the men found themselves. Meyerhold's biomechanical monism was more rigorous than Stanislavsky's version, for it was Pavlovian, holding that the psychological was fundamentally a manifestation of the physical. Pavlov, in *Conditioned Reflexes: An Investigation of the Physiological Activity in the Cerebral Cortex*, defines behavior as a series of reflex responses to stimuli, like a psychophysical chain in which one reflex unfolds into another and then another (Pavlov 1927: 9–10). This definition parallels Meyerhold's description of the acting cycle, in which intention (or preparation) leads to realization (performance of the action) and thence to reaction (which becomes a new intention, or moment of preparation) (Meyerhold 1969: 201). The principles underlying this cycle posit sequences of reflexes as "the neurophysiological basis of complex behaviors" (Roach 1993: 203). Both Meyerhold's and Pavlov's theories, which can be seen as theories of enchainment, or flow, operate on a relatively gross level, but they have elements that are analogous to the "unbroken line," "continuous being," and mental "filmstrip" that Stanislavsky describes in *An Actor Prepares*, and, on a micro level, to the way synapses fire. All of these relate to associative, or unfolding, views of behavior that presage some of the work now being done by scientists who are examining the relationship between neural processes and psychophysiological response. Two vivid connections can be made between the Russians of the 1920s and 1930s, and scientists working today. Psychologist Jerome Kagan describes psychological development as "a sequence of cascades involving large numbers of events" (Kagan 2001: 187), while neuroscientist Antonio Damasio describes how emotions and feelings are a series of enchained psychophysiological responses that rise to the level of awareness by virtue of being attached to images (Damasio 1999: 291). It is impossible to know what Stanislavsky and Meyerhold would have thought of this work, but these people have in common their sense of human experience as a sequence of actions and reactions in the organism, connected to imagery, operating on both conscious and unconscious levels. As Meyerhold said, "The contemporary director must know not only the direct impact of an actor's emotion—he steps to the footlights and brilliantly delivers a soliloquy—but also the complex and peripheral turns of associative imagery" (quoted in Gladkov 1997: 126).

The concept of associations—of the connections we make among various aspects of our experience—was central to Meyerhold's theory. One aspect of this is exemplified by his interest in the James-Lange theory's description of the associations among stimuli, behavior, and emotion/feeling and to which Meyerhold could have had access as early as 1898 through Ribot's writings (Roach 1993: 201). James-Lange had resonance with principles already articulated by Ivan Sechenov, and it provided a core principle of Meyerhold's approach. This theory posits that action, in response to stimuli, precedes feeling, so that the sequence of events that one experiences is not "I see the bear, I feel frightened, I run," but rather "I see the bear, I run, I feel frightened." That is, feeling follows action, based on stimulus. This is in some ways a rough precursor of Damasio's somatic marker hypothesis, and it can also be illustrated by "I'm heading for a car wreck, I narrowly miss the car wreck, I feel frightened" (think for a moment about what actually happens in this common experience). In fact, as early as 1863 Sechenov defined fright as a reflex that follows the initial muscular response to a stimulus (Roach 1993: 201). Another manifestation of the influence of this theory on Meyerhold is in his quest for associative parallels among stimuli and behavior to evoke "the enormous power of imagery in the theatre," described in the quotation that opens this section.

Though in the early 1920s Meyerhold, being a good Communist, was vocal in his skepticism about things having to do with the soul (or at least he talked a good game) and adhered to a strict materialist view, he nonetheless was united with Stanislavsky in viewing the body as inseparable from the mind and in asserting that the actor's work depended on developing a meticulous score that married intention with physicality Both believed there were automatic parts of organic processes that were beyond the control of the conscious self, but that these ultimately could be guided by conscious technique. In Meyerhold's case, this technique was quintessentially physical and it was for the purpose of facilitating the proper state of "excitation"—or engagement or presence—in the actor:

> A theatre built on psychological foundations is as certain to collapse as a house built on sand. On the other hand, a theatre which relies on certain *physical elements* is at very least assured of clarity. [. . .] By correctly resolving the nature of his state physically, the actor reaches the point where he experiences the *excitation* which communicates itself to the spectator and induces him to share in the actor's performance [. . .] It is this excitation which is the very essence of the actor's art.
>
> (Meyerhold 1969: 199)

Though many training programs and teachers set up Meyerhold and Stanislavsky as being diametrically opposed to each other, their similarities are at least as important as the differences, if not even more so. Both men were deeply engaged with questions of the psychophysiology of the performer. Both based elements of their methods on the work of researchers such as Ribot, Pavlov, James, and Lange because these provided an integrated way of thinking about the relationship among body, mind, and feeling. For both, the body was central to the work.

The Americans who were influenced by and appropriated Russian approaches to actor training beginning in the 1920s had little acquaintance with Meyerhold. Stanislavsky was their main source. And while they differed from Stanislavsky in some of their views and tended to sideline the body in some ways, each in his or her own way drew on principles of association and psychophysiology in order to achieve the goal of a truthful, immediate performance in ways that would have been familiar to the Russian masters.

The Americans

[. . .] you touch the things, in your mind, but with the senses
alive. And we know from psychology that emotions have a
conditioning factor. That's how we're trained, not from Freud,
but from Pavlov. The emotional thing is not Freud, as people
commonly think. Theoretically and actually, it is Pavlov. By
singling out certain conditioning factors, you can arouse certain
results.

(Lee Strasberg to Richard Schechner,
in Munk 1967: 198)

The introduction of Stanislavsky-based approaches to acting in the
US began with the founding of the American Laboratory Theatre
(1923–1930) by Richard Boleslavsky who, along with Maria
Ouspenskaya, taught what they had learned from Stanislavsky while
members of the Moscow Art Theatre company in its earliest years.
Among Boleslavsky's students were Lee Strasberg, Harold Clurman,
and Stella Adler. Strasberg and Clurman, along with Cheryl
Crawford, founded the Group Theatre (1931–1941), of which
Adler, Sanford Meisner, and Robert Lewis were members. All went
on to have a major impact on American theatre and actor training.
Most significant among the teachers were Strasberg at the Actors
Studio, where he taught from 1948–1982, Meisner at the Neigh-
borhood Playhouse from 1935–1997, and Adler at the Stella Adler
Theatre School from 1949–1992. These three and Stanislavsky, in
the highly edited versions that till now have been our primary
English-language sources, collectively defined the primary terrain
of American acting for the latter half of the twentieth century.

Their various methods remain the foundation for much of how
acting is taught in the US. Though there are significant variations
among them, the American master teachers had the same goal for
the actor that Stanislavsky did: to "live truthfully," emotionally and
physically, in imaginary circumstances. Stanislavsky described the
actor's fundamental aim as "the creation of [the] inner life of a
human spirit, and its expression in artistic form," which the actor
accomplishes by "living the part" (Stanislavsky 1936: 14) through
using techniques to reach the unconscious by conscious means. Lee
Strasberg stated that the purpose of his exercises was "to train the
actor's sensitivity to respond as fully and vividly to imaginary
objects on stage as he is already capable of doing to real objects in
life" (Strasberg 1988: 123). Sanford Meisner's exercises "were

designed to strengthen the guiding principle that [he] learned forcefully in the Group [Theatre]—that art expresses human experience" (Meisner 1987: 11). Key to this for Meisner is what he calls "true emotion"; this was embodied in a performance in *Magda* by Eleanora Duse, in which she really blushed—for him, "the epitome of living truthfully under imaginary circumstances, which is my definition of good acting" (Meisner 1987: 15). For Stella Adler it was crucial that "You must be truthful in what you do or say. Feel the truth within yourself. The most important thing is for the actor to sense his own truth" (Adler 1988: 12); Adler was also careful to note that the actor had to distinguish between "the truth of life and the truth of the theatre" (Adler 1988: 7). These teachers manipulated principles of action, imagination, attention, and affective and sense memory to help the actor reach what Stanislavsky called the "inner creative state"—a complete engagement with the work. "Truth" and "living the part" are loaded terms, but I cite them here in their historical usage and as a way of pointing to an experience or sense of engagement and presence. (Joseph Roach's article "It" is particularly useful in its discussion of presence and the problems of that term.)

Like Stanislavsky, Strasberg, Adler, and Meisner each start with something other than feeling or emotion. For Meisner, "The foundation of acting is the reality of doing" (Meisner 1987: 16), or action, specifically and crucially in relation to a scene partner. Adler emphasized given circumstances, imagination, and physical actions; for her the key is the actor's imagination in relationship to the given circumstances of the play, so that the actor must choose images that "*evoke an inner feeling,*" connected to those given circumstances (or story/narrative elements). The key elements for Strasberg were relaxation, concentration, and affective memory, which is remembering in meticulous detail a situation that evokes a desired feeling. All of these terms and techniques relate to specific kinds of stimuli connected to what has happened in the past or what is happening now in the actor's environment or experience, invoked for the purpose of engaging the actor with the play's material. Thus, in spite of the slipperiness of the goal—"emotional truth"—, the methods employed are concrete and emphasize the material and physical aspects of the actor's problem.

All three of the American teachers follow Stanislavsky's dictate that "*all action in the theatre must have an inner justification, be logical, coherent and real*" (Stanislavsky 1936: 46), thereby placing

the central element of the actor's work in line with basic characteristics of consciousness that allow us to negotiate our daily lives.
Imagination is the thing that allows us to situate ourselves by
connecting ourselves to our immediate, past, and future environments and, without it, consciousness doesn't exist. Various uses of
imagination provide the ground for all of the American methods
and, thus, these methods are at their core relational, for imagination
is always about the individual having a relationship with some
kind of internal or external object. The Americans' methods are
permeated by metaphors—images, if you will—of the body, locus,
and agency (in a manner similar to that described by Lakoff and
Johnson). The use of given circumstances (e.g., Adler's "who,"
"what," "where"), of action vividly imagined and enacted (the
foundation of Meisner's approach), and of objects and experience
(in Strasberg) is an extension of this fundamental structure of human
consciousness. In all of these approaches, imagination, used for the
purpose of constructing a narrative that drives the action, is central.
Imagination is a, if not *the*, key term that provides a link between
acting and cognitive neuroscience.

An entry point

An accessible, though not unproblematic, way to begin applying
the current cognitive neuroscience to acting is to use Steven Pinker's
computational model of mind, described in *How the Mind Works*.
This schematic model relies significantly on the earlier generation
of computer-influenced theories of cognition, making it somewhat
reductive; however, its schematic nature is precisely what makes it
an easy entry point for connecting science and acting, particularly
in the way it allows us to draw analogies between some key terms
in the two disciplines. The computational theory posits that we
behave in certain ways because we process information based on a
genetic program that determines how we develop and learn. For
Pinker, "Behavior is an outcome of an internal struggle among many
mental modules, and it is played out on the chessboard of opportunities and constraints defined by *other* people's behavior" (Pinker
1997: 42). This behavior is adaptive, designed to allow the organism
to prevent or accomplish something, while negotiating obstacles,
i.e., it is action in the actor's sense. According to this model, we have
several kinds of representation in our heads—most importantly,
visual images, grammatical representations (spoken language), and

mentalese (a term Pinker uses to describe a pre- or meta-verbal "language" of thought that carries information and that we might relate to terms such as "impulse" or "instinct"). This allows spatial relationships and matters of force or power to appear in the mind as mental representations, or symbols. These mental representations—which is almost too concrete a way of describing them—have both representational and causal properties, i.e., they carry information and motivate behavior. Another way of putting it is that these symbols have both narrative (informational) and dramatic (behavioral) aspects.

This perspective, which emphasizes symbolic representations, views the brain less in terms of unmediated stimulus-response (akin to principles of associationism, reflexology, or behaviorism that view the organism mechanistically from a pre-cognitive science perspective) and more in terms of a field of conscious and subconscious internal representations (Pinker 1997: 109). Consciousness is composed of the awareness of a rich field of sensations, i.e., a very generalized sensory awareness, much of which operates pre- or unconsciously, that becomes refined as portions of this sensory information fall under what Pinker calls "the spotlight of attention" (Pinker 1997: 140); whether something falls under this spotlight depends on its importance to our interest and well being. This becomes the material of mental representations and resonates closely with acting concepts such as circle of attention and point of concentration in the various acting systems. In acting, these key concepts are connected not only primarily to vision, but also to the other senses, especially in Strasberg's sensory exercises, and they relate to how the organism negotiates its environment, or "given circumstances," in order to maximize its ability to prioritize and accomplish its goals. Stanislavsky prefigures this approach when he describes the link between attention, interest or desire, and creativity, noting that the actor can trigger creativity by collecting and focusing attention on an interesting object (Stanislavsky 1936: 89). In the computational theory, the main features of consciousness are "*sensory awareness, focal attention, emotional coloring, and the will*" (Pinker 1997: 136, italics in original), which are processed as a series of mental representations. These traits are aligned with Stanislavsky's three inner motive forces—mind, feeling, and will (Stanislavsky 1936: 244–251), and principles of sense memory and observation, concentration, attention to emotion, and action. In short (and obviously), inherent features of human functioning

So Pinker/computational "="
Stanislavski, even this the latter's
The twentieth-century heritage 43

provide the actor with a technique for constructing a string of
symbols in order to trigger things to happen in the body, i.e., to *behaviorist?*
access the unconscious by conscious means. [These representations
are a kind of formulation, and hence a filtering, of experience,
involving a high degree of selectivity, both conscious and unconscious.] Since these symbol sets are intensely individual perceptions
or interpretations of phenomenal experience, it means that the
correlative nature of mental representations works in highly
personal and individualized ways. The implications of this go
beyond a conventional, individually-based, "psychotherapeutic" or
"psychoanalytic" interpretation, for the computational model
describes one possible way to visualize how the mind filters and
transforms experience by connecting sense data and past experiences
through stringing together sets of symbols.

Pinker's concepts of focal attention, behavior, information, and
mental representations are particularly useful in illuminating
our understanding of the repetition exercise, the cornerstone of
Meisner's method. The repetition exercise demands that actors
closely observe and respond to what they are receiving from the
other performer—seeing and listening to the other person in the
space in a focused, moment-by-moment way. This exercise is rooted
in the principles of concentration and directed activity (focal
attention and behavior), given circumstances (information),
and imagination (mental representations). Built on focusing on an
activity and responding meticulously to a scene partner, the
repetition exercise can facilitate immediacy and emotional specificity
in a relationship and help the actor to penetrate what Pinker
describes as an evolutionary "firewall" between "reasonable" and
"emotional" behavior, allowing the actor to break through
habituated conditioning and behave with emotional and theatrical
spontaneity. Meisner distinguishes between "instinct"—the source
of good acting—and "the head"—the source of bad acting, con- *ouch*
stantly reiterating, "Don't think—do" in his book. This approach
is easy to categorize as anti-intellectual, which it no doubt is, but
Meisner's method is effective in getting actors to move from planned
("the head") to impulsive ("instinctive") response. Rather than just
dismiss Meisner's approach as anti-intellectual, I prefer to think of
it as giving priority to action, given circumstances, and responsiveness, rather than to planning, in the moment of performance;
from this perspective, the psychophysical rightness of his method
is clear.

Adler of course is similar to Meisner, but her approach is significantly different in its emphasis on the text and the actor's imaginative engagement with it, focusing concentration on the script's given circumstances. The emphasis on the character's engagement with given circumstances not only reflects Adler's emphasis on the sociological dimensions of theatre, connected to her sense of larger social issues and their impact on human behavior, coming out of her experience in the 1920s and 1930s, it also mirrors Pinker's description of how the organism engages its environment through developing mental representations of its actual and its possible, imagined engagement with its situation. Adler's technique is in line with this, for the key to unlocking the actor's power requires the actor to do a detailed inventory of information found in the script in order to construct vivid, personal mental representations related to the character's story. (The centrality of mental representations and imagination will be considered in more detail in later chapters.)

Strasberg has consistently been called emotionally indulgent and seen as demanding an unhealthy narcissism and egocentricity from his actors. He has been rejected by Adler and Meisner for more than a few reasons, but particularly in regard to his emphasis on "affective memory" (Meisner 1987: 10). Interestingly, while there are genuine grounds for criticism, fundamental elements in Strasberg are in line with current cognitive neuroscience research. Perhaps most significant is that Strasberg begins his work with actors with relaxation and then with attention to objects; he is adamant about not beginning with feelings. His exercises involve the actor concentrating first on physical objects (such as a coffee cup), after which they move on to concentrate on internal ones (such as a memory). We tend to fixate on Strasberg's emphasis on affective memory, which is sometimes misconstrued as the actor remembering a feeling or recapturing an affect. In fact, Strasberg's affective memory technique focuses the actor on remembering a *situation* in all of its vivid, sensory details, which evokes a rich nexus of images that then facilitates a feeling response; this builds directly on the actor's earlier practice in concentrating on physical and then internal objects. At its core, Strasberg's approach is material:

> The sequence [of exercises in the Method] was not arrived at casually, but contains a basic logic derived from practice and experience. The sequence proceeds from the simple to the more complex; from objects that are in our immediate environment

to objects that reside only in our memory; from objects that are external and clearly observable to objects that are internal and depend on our inner concentration to be recreated. We move from single objects of attention to combinations of a number of objects. Thus, the actor is prepared for the variety of problems that he will have to deal with in the scene and in the play.

(Strasberg 1988: 124)

All of the Americans, like Stanislavsky, begin with information. For all of them, feeling follows and grows out of something with sensory dimensions—an object, internal or external, whether it is an image from a memory, the feeling of the coffee cup in the hand, the look on a fellow actor's face—and the associations that the actor has with this. All of these teachers were about facilitating the actor's dynamic engagement with her environment through working with and through the body—the senses—as the source of imagination, in a way that acknowledged the actor's experience as being simultaneously, inseparably imaginary and real.

Current developments in the science of acting

Now the question is: how can one produce, at-will, a certain emotion, control its beginning and ending, and at the same time, transmit it vividly to an audience? [. . .] During improvisations or rehearsal situations, the actor can use his/her own emotions, which have their own natural time course. At certain points in rehearsal, however, and/or during an actual performance, he/she needs to move at will from one emotion to another according to a predetermined evolution of the dramatic situation.

(Bloch 1993: 122)

Experimental psychologist Susana Bloch's research into emotion in relationship to acting represents a significant late twentieth/early twenty-first-century application of science to actor training. Though her impact in the US is not comparable to that of others I have discussed, her application of psychology and physiology places her firmly in the tradition of those who have used science to understand and shape the actor's process. In 1970 in Santiago, Chile, Bloch began an interdisciplinary research project with neurophysiologist Guy Santibañez and theatre director Pedro Orthous in order to study the connections among physiological, expressive, and subjective components of emotions, echoing aspects of Stanislavsky's work with psychophysical technique, but specifically focusing on the actor's use of emotion. Two of Bloch's primary interests in regard to acting were Diderot's assertion in *Paradoxe sur le comedien* that the actor's job is not to feel an emotion, but to duplicate as powerfully as possible the external signs of feeling so that the audience is moved; and the challenge which the actor faces in duplicating as consistently as possible these "external signs." Her concern to help actors access the manifestation of selected emotions is similar to some elements in Stanislavsky, Strasberg *et al.*, but there are significant differences. Bloch defines emotions as "distinct and dynamic functional states of the entire organism, comprising particular groups of effector systems (visceral, endocrine, muscular) *and* particular corresponding subjective states (feelings)" (Bloch 1993: 123). That is, emotions are physiological states of arousal, not cognitively defined perceptions of feelings; in this regard, Bloch is in line with Damasio, LeDoux, and others in the neural and cognitive sciences. Bloch and her collaborators' experiments focus on manipulating actors to generate particular and controllable physical states of emotion; their research posits that specific emotions are linked to specific "patterns of breathing, facial expression, degree of muscular tension, and postural attitudes" (Bloch 1993: 124). Though the term "emotional state" is also used by some acting teachers to describe an actor playing a generalized feeling of, say, happiness or outrage, rather than focusing on specific elements of a scene, Bloch's "emotional state" means something very different, for it refers to a carefully articulated physiological response, not its translation into a non-specific feeling "label."

Bloch's ALBA Emoting technique, based on her work with actors in the laboratory, has been practically applied in a number of settings, and is being taught in a few programs in the US. The technique allows the actor to access and produce primary emotional states by duplicating what she calls emotional effector patterns, which are "scientifically measured patterns of breath, facial expression, and muscle tone" (Rix 1993: 55). Since all of these—breath, face, and body stance—are components of emotions, Bloch theorizes that the more elements an actor activates in her emotional arsenal, the closer the actor's "emotional output" will be to "natural emotions" (these are Bloch's terms). The ALBA technique guides the actor through duplicating a precise score of the physiological and muscular states of six emotions or conditions—fear, sadness, anger, joy, eroticism, tenderness—, generally organized along axes of withdrawal/approach and tension/relaxation. Following the arousal of emotion induced by these patterns, the actor engages in a process of "stepping out," i.e., leaving the induced emotional state by performing another, re-balancing pattern. This work is in the tradition of the theories of reflexologists and behaviorists from the early twentieth century, including the James-Lange theory, for it approaches emotion and behavior materially and quantifiably, rather than psychoanalytically and qualitatively. Bloch also draws on the path-breaking work, begun more than a quarter-century ago and still ongoing, of Paul Ekman, who has conducted global studies of facial–emotional expressiveness. Ekman's research has revealed that emotional responses are universal, i.e., basic emotional states such as fear and happiness look and feel the same worldwide; what differs culturally and individually are the things that trigger the emotions and the ways that we deal with and interpret them. This research operates on the psychobiological, as well as the psychological and social, levels.

Roxane Rix, a certified teacher of ALBA Emoting, describes the work as having a number of phases. The initial phase is "robotic," involving repetition of the patterns with a focus on technical accuracy; this includes learning to control muscles that are normally part of only autonomic processes. According to Rix and Bloch in the second phase, "induction," genuine emotions begin to be induced, emerging from practicing the patterns without being connected to typical emotion stimulus or conscious cognitive content. The idea that emotions can exist apart from conscious content might be difficult for actors to grasp at first, but this is fundamental to understanding the current science, which defines emotions as body states, while feelings are consciously registered "interpretations" of these body states. In the third phase, the ALBA Emoting technique allows actors to replicate specific, physical states involving breath, posture, and face, separate from, but in the service of, what might be called character and given circumstances, which the actor then registers and interprets in subjective terms to connect them to the given material. This process is an embodiment of the paradox, or duality, of the actor's spontaneity: the effector patterns are repeated so that they become automatic or habituated, i.e., organically spontaneous, thereby freeing the actor to be consciously spontaneous and impulsive in the moment. (Roach discusses this dual sense of spontaneity at length.)

Bloch's technique is a precise way of manipulating the body and breath to arouse a "real" emotional state, which is accurately perceived by the audience. (This research should be studied even more deeply in light of current research on mirror and simulation neurons.) In addressing this component of the actor's work, ALBA Emoting supports aspects of the actor's process that follow and build on preliminary research, analysis, and, it could be argued, initial improvisations. ALBA Emoting is a powerful tool for consciously generating emotions, and it can be a useful adjunct to Stanislavsky-based work. Since this technique is for the purpose of helping the actor produce, simulate, and manage emotions, it does not address character research and text analysis; rather, it is a tool for exploring and expanding upon that research. In this regard it is a supplement to, rather than a competitor against, Stanislavsky-based methods. Some may want to argue that ALBA Emoting is in fact opposed to one of Stanislavsky's central principles—that one cannot start with the emotion, but must start with consciously controllable means such as imagination and action, connected to the text's given circumstances. However, this is a misunderstanding based upon the ambiguities of vocabulary and the nebulousness of much of our language for describing subjective experience. "Emotion" for Stanislavsky is what Damasio, Bloch, and others would call "feeling" within the contemporary neurocognitive paradigm, i.e., the conscious experience of a body state, or the subjective interpretation of that body state as positive or negative in relationship to one's current situation and past experience. For Bloch *et al.*, an emotion is the body state itself, and therefore to some degree it is consciously controllable. (Anyone who meditates will understand the distinction.)

ALBA Emoting opens up a new perspective on questions about the nature of emotion, acting, and subjective "truth" whose roots can be traced back as far as Diderot and even the ancient Roman Quintilian, for it is now possible to treat aspects of the physiological processes involved in the generation and "channeling" of emotional states in objective, even quantifiable, ways. It potentially leads to a reassessment of the actor's purpose in (re)producing emotions, for what are the place and meaning of emotions for the actor, if they are generated apart from narrative content and personal feelings? What is authentic about weeping, if it is generated solely through physical self-manipulation? And should this matter? The philosophical issues raised by Bloch's work are considerable.

Dutch research psychologist Elly Konijn approaches the issue of the actor's feelings from what she calls a psychological task-based perspective. In *Acting Emotions: Shaping Emotions on Stage* and "The Actors Emotions Reconsidered," based on her own experience as an actor-in-training, research in the history of acting theories, and interviews with Dutch and US actors, Konijn has devised a four-tier schema for understanding actors' feelings (Konijn uses the term "emotions," but for consistency's sake I will stay with Damasio's and Bloch's use of the term "feelings" to describe the conscious dimensions of affective experience):

Levels of enactment	Levels of feelings
private person	private feelings
actor-craftsman	task-feelings
inner model	intended feelings
performed character	character-feelings
	(Konijn 1997: 33)

This research is interesting for its documentation of the way in which actors talk about their experiences and processes; the descriptions of double-consciousness will be familiar to most performers. However, a number of assumptions forming the foundation of Konijn's assessment risk perpetuating notions that have historically hampered the actor's ability to work holistically and organically. Used judiciously, the "levels" schema is a useful framework for targeting a given issue in rehearsal or performance and for allowing one to shift perspective (it can be an effective shorthand in rehearsal to speak of "this" as being "me" and "that" as being "the character"), but this model continues a split way of thinking about the actor's relationship to the character; it perpetuates a view of the character as an entity, rather than a construct or, better yet, a process; and it presents self-reporting as a valid methodology with scientific uses, without material corroboration or a critical assessment of the cultural and personal assumptions supporting it. While Konijn's study is engaging in approaching feelings anecdotally, it does not address the psychophysiology of emotions as Bloch does, and it does not look at the neurocognitive processes out of which feelings and action arise. The problem of tapping in to or performing feelings is only one component of the actor's work. Konijn's research stops at the level of conscious mind and selective psychological measurements, and is on the verge, at least implicitly, of viewing emotions as objects or categories, rather than processes. Because Konijn doesn't address the neurobiological ground of what the actor is doing, her approach cannot address the "blur" between actor and character, e.g., the not-me/not-not-me involved in play, described by D. W. Winnicott and used by Victor Turner, Richard Schechner, and others in describing the phenomenon of performance since at least the early 1970s (see, e.g., Schechner 1985: 109–110, and Turner 1982: 120–121).

The following chapter addresses aspects of current cognitive neuroscience and their implications for Stanislavsky-based approaches to performance, particularly in how we might integrate our uses of body, feeling, intellect, imagination, and spirit in new and compelling ways for the actor.

Chapter 3

A way of thinking about acting

There is that in me—I do not know what it is—but I know it
   is in me . . .
Do I contradict myself?
Very well then I contradict myself,
(I am large, I contain multitudes.)

(Walt Whitman 1975: 123)

The Brain—is wider than the Sky—
For—put them side by side—
The one the other will contain—and You—beside—

(Emily Dickinson 1960: 312)

Art is a product of the imagination [. . .] In this process
imagination plays by far the greatest part.

(Konstantin Stanislavsky 1936: 54)

Stanislavsky spoke of the actor's task as being "the creation of
[the] inner life of a human spirit," "reaching the subconscious by
conscious means," "the artistic embodiment of inner emotional
experience," and "living [experiencing through] the part." In the final
incarnations of his work, informed by his research in Ribot and
James-Lange, Stanislavsky's goal was to guide the actor to create
an embodied, coherently articulated, expressive being, through a
close engagement with the given circumstances of the script and
the production (i.e., the "who," "where," "when," "what," and
the specific language) and the manipulation of attention, imagination, memory, and behavior. This meticulous work was in the
service of helping the actor more consistently tap into what Stanislavsky called "inspiration" and "creativity," and what we might

also call "flow" or "presence"—the sense of the actor fully inhabiting the role and the moment. The actor's work is akin to that of the dancer's or the musician's, for each memorizes a score, whether it is textual, choreographic, or musical, that engages and interacts with the body. The same text or score may be memorized word for word, step for step, or note for note by different artists, but the way in which the score is executed will vary greatly from individual to individual; both Mstislav Rostropovich and Yo-Yo Ma play Bach's cello suites beautifully, but they also play them differently, because there are two different consciousnesses and bodies informing the performances. At the heart of every performance is a complex consciousness that inhabits the entire body, in which voluntary processes are inseparable from involuntary ones and in which genetic predisposition is inseparable from personal history.

One way of defining successful performances are those in which each note, gesture, or word feels fully connected to the overall flow of the piece; this is the application of technical specificity in the service of psychophysical spontaneity, that is, if you find the right "score," the feeling will follow. This is essentially the approach described by Vasily Toporkov in *Stanislavski [sic] in Rehearsal*, a recounting of his experience being taught and directed by Stanislavsky from 1927 to 1938. The value in this approach, which involves moving from an overview of the entire play and its throughline of action to an engagement with each of its components in meticulous detail, can be taken into its next "generation" by connecting it to cognitive neuroscience. This is also true of the variations in Meisner, Adler, and Strasberg *et al.* In a nutshell, this is the path that the work follows: get a clear picture of the entire play and its movement through the scenes; be word-specific in memorizing the text (i.e., treat it like Shakespeare, even if it isn't); work with particular and personal images in constructing the unfolding action; be open to amendments and refinements; leave no moment "unfilled," "unconnected," or unquestioned. Dig deeply. This is simple (even simplistic) and in some way restates what others have said before. But what differs are both some elements of technique and also, more importantly, a transformed way of thinking about imagination and action, based in a knowledge of the neuro-cognitive ground of memory, feeling, and imagery.

Just as acting is a process of research, trial and error, and refinement in the studio and on stage, neurocognitive theories and strategies come out of research, out of work in the laboratory or operating room, and, hence, they are always provisional and subject to revision. There are scientific principles and laws, but variability must also be taken into account, new discoveries are constantly being made, and there is often substantial variation in the interpretation of the meaning of those discoveries. The process of good science mirrors that of the best acting teachers, including Stanislavsky, who was always revising his thinking based on his research and his experience with actors and singers in the studio. The body, our biological being, which Elizabeth Wilson has called "a site of play" (Wilson 1998: 96), is at the core of this. Since consciousness is a result of the dynamic interaction between the body and the environment, including culture, psychology—a phenomenon of the body—has a location that "must always and everywhere be undermined by mobility" (Wilson 1998: 188–189). At the core of our biological processes and fundamental to evolutionary development is the seeming paradox that human development is both constrained (by inherited and environmental factors) and contingent (because the results of the interactions of those factors can never be fully predicted or predetermined). There is no strict determinism in the relationship between biological developments and the thoughts, feelings, and behavior that emerge from them; rather, we are constrained within certain, sometimes broad, parameters by biology and experience which interact with each other. According to psychologist Jerome Kagan, biological processes set up biases in us to develop in certain ways, so that each person's make-up provides the potential for "a certain *family* of developmental outcomes," rather than a singular trajectory for a life (Kagan 2001: 177, emphasis added). For Kagan, human psychological development is like a "a sequence of cascades involving large numbers of events. Each event decreases, or limits, the probability of developing some outcomes, while determining no specific outcome" (Kagan 2001: 187). Similarly, biological anthropologist Terrence Deacon describes human development in the broader evolutionary scale in this way:

> [. . .] evolution doesn't just build things up like a recipe. It sets up a stage of competition and then lets that competition set up another stage of competition, which then sets up another stage; in a sense, this is evolution inside of evolution inside of evolution.
>
> (Harrington *et al.* 2001: 248)

That is, species develop through stages of competition, while individuals develop through cascades of experience, through a persistent, contingent interaction between the organism and the environment; this can be compared metaphorically to the way a character works on and is affected by her given circumstances.

In the view of science, mind is often viewed as "a process, not a thing" (Damasio 1999: 183). Biology and psychology operate dynamically, and this view permeates cognitive neuroscience's definitions of consciousness and mind. Some people conflate mind and consciousness, but they are in fact not synonymous. Only consciousness and *conscious* mind are the same thing. Many, and in fact most, crucial aspects of mind function sub- and unconsciously. And the meaning and scope of what is thought of as the unconscious mind goes far beyond what we think of in the Freudian or psychoanalytic sense; the unconscious also encompasses sensory, kinesthetic, kinesic, and proprioceptive processes. For Joseph LeDoux, consciousness is "the product of underlying [unconscious] cognitive processes" (LeDoux 2002: 191), while mind is "an integrated system that includes, in the broadest possible terms, synaptic networks devoted to cognitive, emotional, and motivational functions" (LeDoux 2002: 258). This means that the "self," insofar as it is something we experience, is dynamic and fluid; or, as LeDoux says, the self is "not real, though it does exist," for it is "the totality of what an organism is physically, biologically, socially, and culturally. Though it is a unit, it is not unitary. [. . .] the self is a 'dramatic ensemble'" (LeDoux 2002: 31). Emily Dickinson and Walt Whitman were right: the brain is wider than the sky, and each of us contains multitudes.

Culture and the construction of feeling

It is possible to have a range of ways of comprehending how consciousness and language might arise out of the simultaneously constrained and provisional interactions of biology and culture. Kagan describes four types of psychological structures in humans to provide one way of understanding how this happens. The first kind of structure encompasses representations of bodily activity, or visceral representations, that contain information about physiological states, e.g., digestion and respiration; the second includes representations of motor sequences, or sensorimotor schemes, i.e., these are "reports" about movement that allow us to orient ourselves in space and move effectively (this is what makes it possible for us to learn to walk and run and then not have to think much about it, and for dancers and musicians to do part of what they do); the third type of structure is composed of schemata about external events, such as those mediated by sight and hearing, i.e., pre-linguistic "reports" about the sensory environment that alert us about things such as the potential for pleasure and danger around us; and the fourth are "semantic structures that combine lexical representations with schemata to form networks that are logically constrained, hierarchical, and used for both thought and communication." The first three kinds of representations have to do with categories of experience, while the fourth has to do with semantic or symbolic systems that allow us to process the first three. It is only in the last category, the topmost level at which deep, organic processes begin to rise to consciousness, that culture consciously comes into play, for semantic structures are the least constrained by biology, since they rely heavily on imagination; we can envision, imagine, and make up language about things that do not have to be even remotely connected to biological experience, and these can therefore vary greatly across cultures and among individuals. A vivid example of how similar biological experiences can be interpreted in substantially different ways based on different semantic categories is evident in a comparison of how Americans and Caroline Islanders tend to classify names for feelings. While both groups make the most important classification according to the categories of "pleasant/unpleasant," there is a major difference in the second most important way these experiences are described; for Americans the second parsing is intensity, i.e. *how* sad or *how* happy we feel, while for Caroline Islanders it is whether another person was the origin of the feeling state. The general psychophysiological states of the two groups are the same, but how these states are interpreted is affected by differing social and cultural structures (Kagan 2001: 179–180).

How we construct our sense of identity and self is greatly affected by the particular semantic categories of social values and the dominant cultural metaphors with which we are raised. The cognitive neuroscience perspective has some similarity to the positions of Judith Butler and others who describe identity as a purely social construction (see, e.g., Butler 1990). However, there are significant differences, for the limitations of biology, including those of our genetic makeup, define specific parameters for the range within which we might develop. We may "contain multitudes," but we don't contain everything. A project of postmodernism from its start has been increasing our awareness of how values are imbedded in a given culture, in its language, imagery, and master narratives. At the conscious level, who we are depends to a great degree on our linguistic interpretations of experience, i.e., on the stories, or narratives, we make up about ourselves and our place in the world; LeDoux discusses this in terms of the idea of a narrative self (LeDoux 2002: 20, 199), while Damasio uses the term "autobiographical self," created from the accrual of memory and conscious experience, to describe the highest level of consciousness (Damasio 1999: 271–272). Since the limitless variability in how experience is interpreted at the level of language and culture has a significant impact on how qualitative and affective aspects of acting are described and valued, actors and acting teachers have to find a different and better way of dealing with the cultural contingency of language structures; a presumption of "truthfulness" or "universality" about a particular linguistic, cultural, or personal framework can unnecessarily limit an actor's creativity. We have to engage culture as conditioned and variable, and to examine its relationship to biology, if we are to get at the actor's process as fully as we might. A point at which biology and culture intersect is in the bodily schema.

Elizabeth Wilson uses the term "bodily schema" to describe the way neural networks, the body, and culture are integrated. This bodily schema is:

> a postural model of ourselves that is dynamic and which determines the *psychological* parameters of bodily posture and movement. New movements are assimilated into one's schema, change that schema, and then become part of the general determining force of bodily posture and movement. Incoming stimuli are always interpreted according to the already existing schemata; thus the registration of every sensation is always influenced by what has gone before. [. . .] Specifically, these schemata are organized chronologically (rather than spatially) and according to various laws of association, and they are mediated by appetite, instinct, interest, and ideals. [. . .] the pattern of interconnections between schemata forms what is called temperament or character. Schemata are also intrinsically

social [. . .] cognition cannot be simply the possession of an individual, but is the effect of a web of determination between individuals, and between an individual and the social.

(Wilson 1998: 171–172)

Bodily schema are an effect of neural networks, which are created and shaped by the whole accumulation of experience and the cognitive processing of that experience. In a general way, the development of neural networks can be understood as the inscription of a certain kind of bodily memory, neural memory, which supports and directs feeling and consciousness. Understanding the function of these neural patterns, even in a general way, helps us better understand a seeming paradox for actors. One of the things that occurs with experience and synaptic patterning is habituation—"a form of learning in which repeated presentation of a stimulus leads to a weakening of response" (LeDoux 2002: 138), i.e., we respond less to a loud noise such as a gunshot or door slamming the more often we hear it. In acting we rehearse and repeat, often in order to achieve the illusion of the first time, with the result that we actually weaken one kind of spontaneous responsiveness, e.g., such as when we react to a gunshot or a slap. This is actually in the service of liberating the other kind of spontaneity. Two things are in fact going on in rehearsal and performance: there is a set score that is repeated within a generalized range of consistency, so that it can be performed "automatically" or "without thinking," and then there is the spontaneous and immediate variation in the enactment of that score in any particular rehearsal or performance. Similarly, a musician might hit the same notes or a dancer might do the same steps night after night, so that the performance is "the same, but different" every time. (Roach discusses this in historical terms.)

So what is it that we are doing when we're acting, or teaching or coaching actors, given the basic questions being raised about consciousness and the self in light of the fluidity and reciprocity of the processes linking brain, mind, culture, and behavior? What happens if we begin to view teaching, training, and rehearsal as a kind of "brain modification" working on both biological and cultural fronts (at least in the sense that any experience modifies the brain)? How does this change our sense of what acting is and the way that it might happen most effectively? At the very least, we have to recognize that three and a half weeks of rehearsal, currently a standard regional theatre rehearsal period, is inadequate for

perhaps bridge practice/research divide? [handwritten marginalia]

allowing the actor to get the work into her body; possibly the importance of time in rehearsal is more obvious and more respected in dance, in which dancers must have enough time to get the work "into their bodies" for sheer safety, as well as all the other aspects of performance preparation. Longer rehearsal periods and runs of a play allow actors more time to develop richer, stronger synaptic patterns and networks by having a longer engagement with a piece of material. The value of these longer processes can be seen, e.g., in the work of Kabuki actors who might play a role for decades or that of the Wooster Group that works on plays for months, sometimes reviving or revising them over the course of years (perhaps the best example of this is their project based on *Three Sisters*, *Brace Up!*). The science provides both an argument for extending rehearsal periods in order to allow the brain and body to do their work and a critique of capitalist theatre models that have to use very brief periods for economic reasons; for plays involving a nuanced, detailed approach to text, three or four weeks is not enough time to inhabit the work sufficiently. An actor who has had time in his work is Sir Ian Richardson; in a summer 2002 master class with John Barton, I saw Richardson recite from *Hamlet*, a role he first played when he was in his twenties. Richardson was then sixty-nine years old, and he did nothing but sit in his chair as he spoke the "To be or not to be" soliloquy. It was a simple, but deeply moving, moment. Richardson's work was supported by not only his skill in the conscious sense, but a deep and ingrained patterning of the synapses in his body and brain. It was a quintessential demonstration of the powerful integration of craft, culture, life experience, and sheer time.

The self

The Russian word for "consciousness" is *samochuvstvo*—literally "self (*sam*)-feeling (*chuvstvo*)," i.e., the feeling, or experiencing, of a self. This Russian reading provides insight into what Stanislavsky might have intended when he centered his work on the idea of an aware and sentient self. The idea of a "self" can be parsed in many ways. In neurocognitive terms the self is multilayered and fluid, real and constructed. LeDoux suggests that "the self of self-awareness is only a part and perhaps only a small part of a broader, objective self that is mostly unconscious or implicit" (LeDoux *et al.* 2003: 1) The explicit self "is not a separable entity, but rather a particular configuration of the implicit, unconscious self" (LeDoux *et al.* 2003: 14). Cognitive neuroscientist Michael Gazzaniga has conducted studies that demonstrate that the mind basically creates a fictional self out of the very small portion of the brain's activities that actually reach consciousness (he asserts that "98% of what the brain does is outside of consciousness awareness" [Gazzaniga 1998: 21]). Our conscious sense of self is necessarily selective and filtered, i.e., "fictional," depending on what story we're trying to tell ourselves:

> There seems always to be a private narrative taking place inside each of us. It consists partly of the effort to fashion a coherent whole from the thousands of systems we have inherited to cope with challenges.
>
> (Gazzaniga 1998: 23)

Psychologist Daniel Wegner even suggests that we "set aside the idea that thoughts [of a fictive self] *cause* actions and instead think about how the mind *attributes* causation of action to itself" (LeDoux *et al.* 2003: 4), i.e., we act, based on many unconscious factors, and attribute motive afterward; this has radical implications for how we might approach scoring a role and particularly for how we might think about character "motivation." Psychologist Daniel Schacter has done research on how "the mind attempts to maintain consistency over time, to preserve the sense of a stable self as author of actions and beliefs," even though beliefs and memories might have radically changed (LeDoux *et al.* 2003: 5). Basically, we construct a self to allow us to "function in a social collective" and to allow our brains to "organize vast arrays of experience into narratives adequate to this functioning" (LeDoux *et al.* 2003: 7–8). Cognitive anthropologist Naomi Quinn says that even cultural knowledge used to construct our "self" is "overwhelmingly implicitly transmitted, and outside conscious self-awareness" (LeDoux *et al.* 2003: 146).

Damasio describes different aspects of self in a way that can illuminate how basic Stanislavskian principles of acting, especially those based on later phases of the work, are embodied in the way our brains are made. For Damasio, the development of a sense of self is the ground from which consciousness derives. His model links the sense of self, consciousness, attention, behavior/action, emotion, and feeling in *physical* ways that have at their core the organism's sense of its relationship to an object; this view has some resonance with Pinker's, but it also has important differences. Damasio addresses the self from a biological perspective, beginning with the proposition that humans are like all other organisms; for all of us, "Survival depends on finding and incorporating sources of energy and on preventing all sorts of situations which threaten the integrity of living tissues" (Damasio 1999: 23). This can be distilled into three necessary things—food, shelter, and protection; without these life cannot continue for long. This is a simple view, but it is not simplistic, for Damasio describes how behavior, intellect, emotion, and imagination support homeostasis in a way that accounts for complexity and contingency. In this relational dynamic, a key function of the brain is to portray "the living organism in the act of relating to an object," which is the ground out of which awareness arises (Damasio 1999: book jacket). Stanislavsky's system fundamentally mirrors this, for it asks the actor to imagine and experience a fictive self engaged with issues of survival or thriving of one kind or another that ultimately involve, affect, and change the body. The actor plays out a variation on Damasio's organism–object relationship in order to embody a character: she takes on some form of the internal (mental) and external objects of the text and its given circumstances, integrates these with her own mental objects, derived from memory and personal history, and devises a pattern of behavior. The result is typically a course of action related to the character's desire to acquire or avoid something. This sketch of what the actor does may be reductive, but it is generally accurate: what characters do is to engage with issues of survival and prosperity in one form or another, whether they be physical, economic, emotional, sexual, or spiritual. Nina in Act IV of *The Seagull* is a quintessential example of a character involved in all of these aspects of survival.

Key attributes of consciousness, which derives from the sense of a self, have correlatives in the vocabulary of the system that allow us to connect the science directly to elements in approaches to acting and character. Among the key terms are self, consciousness, reason, environment, behavior, attention, emotion, feeling, and imagination.

Self is resonant with *character*. For Stanislavsky, an actor successfully embodies a character when she successfully creates "the life of a human spirit" expressed in "a beautiful, artistic form" (Stanislavsky 1936: 14). In more clinical terms, *self* and *character* both refer to an entity that has an awareness of herself, whether in terms of her sense of existing in the world proper or in the world of the play.

Consciousness and *reason* can be connected to points at which a character registers *given circumstances* in a play. Consciousness has to do with the organism's awareness of and ability to respond to the *environment*, which is, ultimately, just another word for given circumstances; these include anything the actor has to take into consideration, such as the play's story, the conditions and history of the play's setting, the particular interpretations being used, and all the physical elements of the production (Stanislavsky 1936: 51). In short—the entirety of all the conditions affecting the actor—character in her immediate and extended environment, especially in relationship to her history and agency.

Behavior is a correlative for *action*, i.e., the organism/character does or attempts certain things out of necessity or desire, in order to negotiate her environment, or given circumstances; "behavior" is, of course, also a word commonly used in film-oriented approaches to acting, to describe the actor's successful replication of naturalistic, non-"theatrical" (even anti-theatrical) activities. All of these refer to a person, character, or organism engaging in some activity that the organism generally experiences as moving itself toward pleasure or comfort and away from pain or discomfort. "Units and Objectives" is how Elizabeth Reynolds Hapgood titles Chapter VII of *An Actor Prepares*, and "define the objective" is a basic task in many acting methods. However, Stanislavsky's word, which Hapgood translates as "objective," is *zadacha*, more accurately translated as "problem" or "task." How might an actor's frame of reference and energy shift, if we spoke of "problem" and "task," rather than "objective"? Action (*deistvie* in Russian) is "What the actor does to solve the problem or fulfill the task set before his or her character by the play" (Carnicke 1998: 169). In Stanislavsky, as in biology, things ultimately come down to the organism taking action to solve problems.

Attention in formal neuroscientific terms means something quite specific: it is what allows the organism to prioritize and engage elements in its environment, sorting through stimuli and focusing on what might affect it positively or negatively. Being able to direct our attention allows us to take care of what matters most, by allowing us to focus our actions and imagination: I may be intently involved in making love, but the smell of smoke or the sound of a gunshot nearby might (and would, I hope) draw my attention and cause me to get out of bed, throw on some clothes, and leave immediately. This parallels Stanislavsky's *point of attention* and *circle of attention* (Stanislavsky 1936: 75, 81): the actor manipulates the direction of her concentration, expanding and contracting her area of focus in Small, Medium, Large, and Largest Circles, centered on a point of attention (an object or event of significance for the character), aided by imagination, in order to pursue the character's objective (or tackle the character's problem) successfully.

Emotion (the preconscious physiological response to a situation, internal or external) and *feeling* (the conscious registration of this body-state), fundamental to consciousness and to acting, are similar in Damasio and Stanislavsky. These will be discussed at length shortly, but for the moment suffice it to say that, for both, feeling is a result or outgrowth of the person's engagement with her given circumstances, her environment.

Even *imagination* is part of our evolutionary survival kit; it has an organic source and serves a pragmatic function. The evolutionary development of the brain links the "world of homeostasis" and the "world of imagination." The former world is that of the biological maintenance of the organism within the narrow parameters within which the body can survive; it has to do with maintaining proper metabolic, endocrine, circulatory, and digestive functions, among others. The latter is that of image-making, in which the organism envisions or projects possible conditions and outcomes that lead it to adjust its behavior to maximize the maintenance of homeostasis, or balance and survival. What this means is that the autonomic drive for homeostasis, i.e., the automatic ways in which our bodies regulate themselves, is fundamental to the biology of consciousness; without the body's homeostatic functions, there would be no source of—or need for—imagination. Imagination is the result of the brain's evolutionary development and is essential to the fact of our physicality, not just our psyches. Actors consistently get at imagination by engaging the senses, e.g., the visual, aural, olfactory, and kinesthetic; we get at imagination and attention through the body. We all have had direct experiences of the link between the imagination and the body, perhaps most obviously evident in basic bodily responses such as blushing, blanching, palpitations, or trembling, which can occur in response to embarrassing or frightening situations, whether these are real or merely imagined. Imagination, in not just its psychological, but also its physical dimensions, is a basic component of consciousness.

Damasio and others posit a kind of proto-narrative as the beginning of consciousness: the organism imagines a rudimentary "story" in which it (the self) encounters something (an object, external or internal) that causes it to react, thereby causing changes in the organism. This begins with something as simple as moving toward pleasure or nourishment and away from pain or danger. It should sound familiar to anyone who has studied Stanislavsky, and especially Meisner, and it parallels theatre's very being as embodied narrative:

> Consciousness begins when brains acquire the power [. . .] of telling a story without words, the story that there is life ticking away in an organism, and that the states of the living organism, within body bounds, are continuously being altered by encounters with objects or events in its environment, or for that matter, by thoughts and by internal adjustments of the life process. Consciousness emerges when this primordial story—the story of an object causally changing the state of the body—can be told using the universal nonverbal vocabulary of [neural and chemical] body signals. The apparent self emerges as *the feeling of a feeling.*
>
> (Damasio 1999: 30–31, emphasis added)

That is, consciousness begins with a preconscious narrative that provides the organism with an elemental story about its basic condition; it arises when the organism begins glimmeringly to become aware of and then registers the feelings of the neural and chemical events of the body, which it uses to define itself—a self— in relationship to objects and events. Stanislavsky-based principles such as through-going action (or throughline of action) and superobjective are all about helping the actor devise an image-based narrative to carry her effectively through the play. The throughline "galvanizes all the small units and objectives of the play and directs them toward the superobjective" (Stanislavsky 1936: 274), which "suggests an overriding action that links together actions throughout the play" (Carnicke 1998: 181). These principles guide the actor to devise a detailed, compelling story to embody through the play.

We do a similar thing in daily life as we continually construct narratives in order to make sense of our experiences and to guide our actions. The science indicates that the human propensity for making stories is more than just a culturally conditioned trait; the process of proto-narrativizing is embedded in brain structure. The continuity of our consciousness is in fact provided by the subterranean flow of nonverbal narratives of what Damasio calls a core consciousness. It is even possible to define consciousness as deriving from "the unified mental pattern [or proto-narrative] that brings together the object and the self"; this means that fundamental organic processes—emotion, feeling, and consciousness—"depend for their execution on representations of the organism," i.e., representations of the body (Damasio 1999: 284). The organism's sense of itself as being a discrete entity either at risk or experiencing pleasure is where consciousness, the sense of self, begins. Consciousness is not an abstract or ethereal process of an incorporeal mind, but a process of the body that helps us negotiate our way through the given circumstances of our lives, in the same way that an actor has to engage a character's given circumstances consciously and physically to determine its course through the play.

Scientists define self and consciousness as existing on a number of levels that provide a structure for being more specific about how actors might use terms such as feeling, emotion, and self. Damasio begins with the *proto-self,* a biological process that underlies consciousness. This self *"is a coherent collection of neural patterns which map, moment by moment, the state of the physical structure of the organism in its many dimensions"* (Damasio 1999: 154). The proto-self has nothing to do with language or self-knowledge. It is a first-order, i.e., "non-translated," preconscious mapping of the organism that allows autonomic responses by basic parts of our biology such as metabolism and reflexes; these are things that lay behind what we "translate" into pleasure, pain, drives, and motivations. Among the brain structures needed to implement the proto-self are the brain-stem nuclei, hypothalamus, and basal forebrain. Our basic awareness of a self grows out of second-order mapping, and is related to a beginning registration of emotions; this is in likelihood generated in some combination of the superior colliculi, the cingulate cortex, and the thalamus. The object image is enhanced by the activation of these sections of the brain responsible for the proto-self and emotions (Damasio 1999: 181). The parts of the brain involved at this level are evolutionarily older and are not sources of conscious functioning, so the actor's conscious use of this level is limited; however, it can be helpful to be aware that this is the ground out of which all conscious functioning grows, and to know that the potentials for conscious mind begin in the body at this level.

Core consciousness is the most basic level of consciousness, and the one on which our awareness at any level depends. Damasio describes this as "the unvarnished sense of our individual organism in the act of knowing":

> You come by this knowledge, this discovery as I prefer to call it, instantly: there is no noticeable process of inference, no out-in-the-daylight logical process that leads you there, and no words at all—there is the image of the thing and, right next to it, is the sensing of its possession by you. [. . .] The essence of core consciousness is the very thought of you—the very feeling of you—as an individual being, involved in the process of knowing of your own existence and of the existence of others.
>
> (Damasio 1999: 126–127)

At this basic level, consciousness is about two things: the engendering of both mental patterns, or images of objects and situations, and the "sense of self in the act of knowing" (Damasio 1999: 9); consciousness is a feeling accompanying the making of an image and the awareness that a self is making, or holding, the image. "Reason" and higher intellectual functions—what Damasio calls *extended consciousness*—grow out of this base of core consciousness. The functions of extended consciousness are centered in the neocortex, the evolutionarily more recent part of the brain. They are built on and cannot exist without the evolutionarily older and inter-dependent functions of the subcortex, core consciousness, and emotion. Representations of emotions, which are essentially balances or imbalances in basic body-states, derive largely from the more primitive, subcortical parts of the brain named earlier, along with the amygdala (Damasio 1999: 79). This overlap with some of the brain structures responsible for the proto-self is one indication of the complex integration of the "layers" of the self: there is no hard and fast biological or physical separation of cognition, emotions, and basic biological operations of homeostasis. While various functions are centered in different parts of the brain, they are neurophysiologically intertwined. (In *Descartes' Error: Emotion, Reason, and the Human Brain*, Damasio describes case studies involving brain-damaged patients that vividly illustrate the inseparability of reason from emotion in the brain's structure.)

Though Stanislavsky's vocabulary is different, his project to connect cognition, imagination, action, emotion, and the body resonates with Damasio's connection of homeostasis to extended consciousness. There is a:

> close linkage between the regulation of life and the processing of images which is implicit in the sense of individual perspective. [. . .] *As for the sense of action, it is contained in the fact that certain images are tightly associated with certain options for motor response.* Therein is our sense of agency—these images are mine and I can act on the object that caused them.
>
> (Damasio 1999: 183, emphasis added)

The strong link between imagination and action in training for the actor are reflected in our very being as a species. Extended consciousness builds on core consciousness to allow us to develop an *autobiographical self* that is composed of a "lived past and antici- pated future," emerging from "the gradual buildup of memories of [. . .] the 'objects' of the organism's biography" (Damasio 1999: 196). Extended consciousness keeps active our personal collection of images of ourselves and the objects we encounter. This can be applied to our understanding of acting: the actor, in a modified and heightened form that involves both core and extended con- sciousness, which manifests in the autobiographical self, brings together and manipulates conscious elements of history, memory, and given circumstances to unlock imagination and responsiveness "in the moment" as effectively as possible.

Emotions and feelings

Damasio's framework for emotion and feeling articulates the different ways in which we might experience things related to our affective and psychophysiological life. Neuroscientists typically use the term "emotion" to describe changes in the neural and chemical condition of the organism, i.e., emotions are changes in the body state and in brain structures that map the body and support thinking. These neural or chemical patterns are produced or changed when the brain detects an emotionally competent stimulus, or ECS, which can be an actual or remembered object whose presence triggers a given pattern. Emotions are automatic, in the sense that they are based on inherited and learned repertoires of action, and, like any bodily process, they are constantly in flux (Damasio 1999: 63). Emotions are of the proto-self and core consciousness, for they are both part of our fundamental, substantially preconscious sense of self and a significant underpinning of the construction of narratives of consciousness. They are biologically determined and depend on specific components and functions of the brain, as encoded by evolution. Though what affects us emotionally can vary significantly, depending on the environment in which we are raised (which includes culture), there is a cross-cultural sameness in emotional response and expression among humans. Paul Ekman's studies in particular document how emotions manifest themselves in facial expressions in the same ways in individuals and groups; though stimuli for a given emotion may differ, based on cultural conditioning, emotional expression in the face is broadly the same, i.e., anger or happiness will generally be recognizable as anger or happiness, regardless of the culture. These studies are another strong evidence that emotions, first and foremost, were and are biological functions, and that we are more similar than different in terms of basic human response.

Emotions' two primary functions in evolution are "[to produce] a specific reaction to an inducing situation [. . . and to regulate] the internal state of the organism such that it can be prepared for the specific reaction." Emotions are a high level but generally preconscious component of life regulation "sandwiched between the basic survival kit (e.g., regulation of metabolism; simple reflexes; motivations; biology of pain and pleasure) and the devices of high reason, but still very much a part of the hierarchy of life-regulation devices" (Damasio 1999: 53–54). Because emotions and core consciousness require many of the same neural substrates, the absence of emotion can often be an indication of a defect in core consciousness and the brain structures that support it. One pervasive indication of the centrality of emotion in all of our lives and its inseparability from "reason" is the way a conscious state *always* has some aspect of emotion—what Damasio calls "background emotion" or what we in theatre might call "mood" or "general state." When we are conscious, there is always something going on with us neurologically and chemically that has an emotional dimension, however low-key or subtle or at the periphery of our awareness; there is no such thing as emotional neutrality. Calmness or mild irritation is as much an emotional state as rage or excitement. It is important for the actor to acknowledge this, for the approach to

the role or rehearsal always grows out of her particular emotional state of the moment.
Feeling is emotion made conscious. Though emotions can exist without consciousness and grow out of aspects of the proto-self, feelings begin when emotions rise to awareness, when the state of the body begins to register consciously in the mind (Damasio 1999: 85). A feeling is *"the perception of a certain state of the body along with the perception of a certain mode of thinking and of thoughts with certain themes"* (Damasio 1999: 86). To use Damasio's apt metaphor, "Emotions play out in the theater of the body. Feelings play out in the theater of the mind" (Damasio 1999: 28). Feelings may in fact be the beginning of what it means to be human, for they could be an essential link between being and knowing, i.e., between mere existence and consciousness (Damasio 1999: 43). Put another way, feeling is how we register and interpret emotions, and consciousness begins with the *"feeling of a feeling."* This is crucial in understanding the nature of feeling in the actor's work. The movement from emotion to conscious feeling is an *enchained* process: the inducer of the emotion (the internal or external object perceived by the organism) produces an automated emotion in neural sites, which leads to a feeling, which leads to the organism *knowing* the feeling, i.e., becoming aware of the feeling in a second-order processing of the encounter with the object (Damasio 1999: 291). This capacity for feeling is what takes us to a uniquely human level in evolutionary development for:

> the process of feeling begins to alert the organism to the problem that emotion has begun to solve. The simple process of feeling begins to give the organism *incentive* to heed the results of emoting [. . .] In turn, knowing is the stepping stone for the process of planning specific and nonstereotypical responses [. . .] In other words, "feeling" feelings extends the reach of emotions by facilitating the planning of novel and customized forms of adaptive response.
>
> (Damasio 1999: 284–285)

Being aware of feelings—the conscious registration of emotions—allows us to be innovative and creative in our responses to the thing causing the emotion, for, at the level of consciousness, choice and decision-making can finally come into play. The great degree of interpretation involved in translating emotional and body states into feeling reinforces the idea that the actor must think creatively and adventuresomely in imagining a role, and in responding to and using emotion and feeling.

Emotions, feelings, thoughts, and behavior become linked over time through associative learning; multivalent networks are developed, activated, and reinforced in such a way that any one aspect can lead the process at any given moment, i.e., a sequence of experience can be initiated by a body state, thought, or gesture. Ekman's studies in facial muscle movement document how physical adjustments lead to shifting emotional and feeling states; these demonstrate that changing the body-state changes the feeling-state, at least in part because of what we consciously associate with a particular body-map. There is also measurable neurological evidence that emotion and feeling sometimes follow "doing"; as Damasio says, "In the beginning was emotion, but at the beginning of emotion was action" (Damasio 1999: 80). (This would no doubt have made Meyerhold happy.) LeDoux supports this stance as well, though he parses the relationship among emotions, feelings, and behavior in slightly different ways. For LeDoux, emotions are a "process by which the brain determines or computes the value of a stimulus," while feelings emerge following the taking of action based on the emotions, i.e., "The feeling of fear came after you jumped and after your heart was already pumping—the feeling itself did not cause the jumping or the pumping" (LeDoux 2002: 206–208). Feeling is basically the organism's conscious interpretation of the response to the stimulus. Both Damasio's and LeDoux's positions provide strong support for Meyerhold's appropriation of the James-Lange theory and for Stanislavsky's methods of physical action and active analysis: by adjusting the body state, by changing physical behavior, the actor can effect and change emotion and, hence, feeling. In this model there is no ground for some of the traditional separations of "reason/ cognition" from "emotion/ feeling" and "viscera" in actor training.

Another aspect of these linkages is that the higher the state of emotional arousal, the higher the number of brain systems that are activated to facilitate responsiveness and learning. This has implications for learning of all kinds, including the kind of "learning" that is done in studios and in rehearsals. The activation of multiple brain systems during emotional arousal allows for significantly greater coordinated learning across those brain systems (LeDoux 2002: 322). That is, the more neurochemically engaged you are as an actor, in terms of sensory and imaginative givens, the better able you will be to engage and explore the scene and to put the work as fully as possible into your body. The connections among emotion, feeling, and memory (which is a kind of learning) bear out the importance of emotional arousal as key to efficacy. In fact, the mood congruity hypothesis posits that it is easier to recall explicit memories by recreating the physical and emotional state at the time of the creation of the memory as much as possible, i.e., by recreating the pattern of activation as much as possible (LeDoux 2002: 222). This provides support for aspects of sense and affective memory, though it is important to place this in the context of the provisional and imaginary nature of memory, for conscious memory is of only relative "authenticity" and has to be viewed carefully in terms of its use for the actor. Ultimately, the point of the affective or sense memory work should be not to "retrieve" the memory, but to support the life of the character lived in the moment of performance—to create a performed, feeling-full present, not a reconstructed past, by activating the actor's organism in the service of the role.

Memory

Memories are fleeting and vivid, nebulous and absolutely real. Sometimes we can't forget even though we want to, and sometimes memories fade, though we want to hold onto them with all our might. Memories are front and center in our consciousness and buried deep below it. But what exactly are they psychophysiologically? And what are they for the actor? In the most basic terms, a memory is a neurochemical event—the activation of a neural pattern. Given that neural patterning is a process of experience, there are key similarities between memory and learning. Both function consciously or unconsciously in a range of ways, whether synaptic, kinesthetic, sensory, or cognitive. The activation of any memory or bit of learning is done through the firing of a set of neuronal connections. Viewing memory as a kind of learning, a kind of patterning and processing of experience, could facilitate a more dynamic and active sense of the use of past experiences by the actor. Though semantic and autobiographical memory are based in different parts of the brain, they are similar in that remembering the multiplication tables and remembering the loss of a loved one both involve the (re)activation of neural patterns; the difference is in the things we consciously associate with them and in the autonomic responses of the body that are activated by the remembering. According to LeDoux:

> Learning, and its synaptic result, memory, play major roles in gluing a coherent personality together as one goes through life. [...] Learning allows us to transcend our genes. [...] Our knowledge of who we are [...] is in large part learned through experience, and this information is accessible to us through memory [...] learning and memory also contribute to personality in ways that exceed explicit self-knowledge. The brain, in other words, learns and stores many things in networks that function outside of conscious awareness.
>
> (LeDoux 2002: 9–10)

Further:

> much of the self is learned by making new memories out of old ones. Just as learning is the process of creating memories, the memories created are dependent on things we've learned before. [... Memory is] a reconstruction of facts and experiences on the basis of the way they were stored, not as they actually occurred.
>
> (LeDoux 2002: 96)

Memories can be categorized as either long-term or short-term, each of which has its own subcategories. There are two kinds of long-term memory: explicit and implicit. Sometimes also called declarative memory, explicit memory is our ability consciously to remember or recall things. It is divided into episodic memory (related to personal experience, i.e., things that have happened to you) and semantic memory (facts, or things you know but have not necessarily experienced, such as the fact that it is winter in New Zealand when it is summer in New York). Because it is relational, inducing one particular explicit memory can lead to the activation of other related memories; this means that explicit memories can be called forth independently from the initial context and stimuli by which they were established (LeDoux 2002: 115). This relational, or conjunctive, characteristic of explicit memory is particularly significant for actors, because of the many ways that associative learning is part of the actor's process; it will be taken up further in the discussion of image streams. Implicit, or procedural, memory has to do with what we do and how we do it, rather than with information we know, i.e., it encompasses learned motor and cognitive skills such as speaking, walking, dancing, or riding a bicycle. Though there is some disagreement about whether "memory" is a term too broadly stretched to encompass conditioned responses, it is being included here, for the actor's work is to construct, embody, and repeat a psychophysical score, and a key element in this is associative conditioning, a kind of habituated learning and patterning. Working memory refers to the ability to remember and to direct our attention to be able to manipulate bits of information. Short-term memory can be considered a subset of working memory, and is the term for remembering things over a very short time, i.e., well under a minute, e.g., as when you get a phone number from the operator and then punch it in. Converting short-term memory into long-term memory can be achieved with rehearsal, repetition, and associative processing, i.e., linking new information with other meaningful memories.

It is common to think of a memory as a set thing, an accurate recollection or representation of something from the past, whether near or distant. We can also think of the act of remembering as the act of retrieving something—an image, a smell, a feeling—that existed in a real or objective way at some point in our history. For most daily purposes this "object retrieval" view is a good enough way of thinking about memory, but numerous studies have shown that memory is extremely unreliable, e.g., whether it is related to eyewitness testimony at a trial or a "retrieved" memory of abuse, memory can often be false or inaccurate. It has been documented over and over again that "memories of emotional experiences are often significantly different from what actually happened during them [. . .] since] memories are constructions assembled at the time of retrieval, and the information stored during the initial experience is only one of the items used in its construction" (LeDoux 2002: 203).

Stanislavsky intuited the transformative and filtering role of time in his thinking about memory and its artistic uses, as described in a conversation between Tortsov and Kostya, the two central characters in *An Actor Prepares* who represent two aspects of Stanislavsky himself, the wise teacher and the questing student:

> "[. . .] Each one of us has seen many accidents. We retain the memories of them, but only outstanding characteristics that impressed us and not their details. Out of these impressions one

large, condensed, deeper and broader sensation memory of
related experience is formed. It is a kind of synthesis of memory
on a large scale. It is purer, more condensed, compact,
substantial and sharper than the actual happenings.
*"Time is a splendid filter for our remembered feelings—
besides it is a great artist. It not only purifies, it also transmutes
even painfully realistic moments into poetry."*
"Yet the great poets and artists draw from nature."
"Agreed. But they do not photograph her. Their product
passes through their own personalities and what she gives them
is supplemented by living material taken from their store of
emotion memories."

(Stanislavsky 1936: 173)

Here, Stanislavsky is beginning to move toward an understanding
of the provisional and mutable nature of memory, moving away
from the problematic technique of emotion (affective) memory. By
the 1930s, realizing the limits and pitfalls of this technique, he
rejected it for more psychophysically oriented approaches. Nonetheless, memory and imagination remained linked in his work.

Memory is intensely fluid and dynamic, and it is crucial for the
actor to come to terms with this in using the activation of memory
as part of her process. Neural reconsolidation is involved in memory retrieval, regardless of the kind of memory. For any memory, a
synaptic pattern needs to be reactivated through a neurochemical
process, i.e., "if you take a memory out of storage you have to
make new proteins (you have to restore, or reconsolidate it) in order
for the memory to remain a memory." Possibly the most radical
corollary of this is that *"the brain that does the remembering is not
the brain that formed the initial memory"* (LeDoux 2002: 161,
emphasis added). Each experience, each thought we have changes
us. It changes our brains. Though most often these changes are
extremely small, it means that, unlike a standard computer model
in which digital paths are set and reproduced exactly time after time
unless they are altered by a person, program, or technical failure,
each time the neural "path" of a memory is reactivated, it is subject
to minor variations based on the accrual of experience and the
particular production of proteins that occurs to facilitate the
remembering at that moment. With each memory, we are in fact remembering—putting back together—a variation on a neural pattern
within a new organic context.

The provisional nature of memory has major implications for how the actor might understand emotion and feeling, particularly in regard to the idea of memory as a reconstruction. Though emotionally competent stimuli "can be actual or recalled from memory" and can trigger a conditioned memory that leads to an emotion, i.e., body state, and thence to a feeling, in the manner of an actor's use of affective or sense memory (Damasio 1999: 57), a memory is not a retrieval of an object. Rather, memory is *"an imaginative reconstruction, or construction, built out of the relation of our attitude toward a whole active mass of past experience"* (LeDoux 2002: 177, emphasis added):

> So memory neither produces something completely new, nor simply reproduces something that already exists. Instead, memory is "literally manufactured" [. . .] within or between already existing schemata. Memory is never the re-presentation of an element stored elsewhere; it is always an "imaginative reconstruction," a constant variation without a discrete origin.
>
> (Wilson 1998: 173)

Two key words here are "imaginative" and "attitude"; our attitudes, which operate consciously and unconsciously, affect the ways in which we imaginatively retrieve and reconsolidate the elements of past experience in restoring a memory. That is, attitude—one could even say "interpretive bias"—directs how we re-member, how we imaginatively reconstruct a memory.

This makes concepts such as affective memory and sense memory not necessarily false, but more complex than they might seem at first glance. As actors we regularly use past emotional and kinesthetic experiences to help connect ourselves more immediately to a character's situation; in much standard actor training this is often seen as reliving an experience or reconstructing an emotional or sensory state to reach a kind of truthfulness and authenticity. However, even though we are reactivating established neural patterns when we have memories, from one perspective they are new events. We are not, in the purest terms, reliving anything; we are having a new experience in the moment, drawing on experiences of the past, shaped by our current condition and imagination. Since memories are "constructions assembled at the time of retrieval" (LeDoux 2003: 203), we must reevaluate traditional approaches in acting to memory, particularly as they relate to feelings. For the actor, as for any person, memory is not a completely accurately retrievable truth, nor is it an object, in the sense of being a "fact." Rather, it is a neuro-chemical reconstruction whose nature is affected by the context in which the retrieval occurs; it is a grasping on to the merest, ephemeral trace, affected by our immediate given circumstances at the moment of the re-membering. If we understand memories as processes, rather than objects, we might more effectively manipulate memory as a tool for acting. We could move simultaneously toward increased specificity and flexibility in our observations, allowing us more emphasis on present-ness and imagination, rather than worrying about accurately "retrieving" a "fact." There is a richer and more productive interpenetration of the biological, psycho-logical, and imaginative than was ever imagined by the master acting teachers.

Rehearsal and performance involve various kinds of "memor-ization"—conscious and unconscious, verbal/vocal, and physical—depending upon the individual actor, the particular theatre piece being done, and the cultural context's impact on these. This opens up a range of approaches for the uses of memory and memoriza-tion in actor training. One possibly not so radical position could hold that, since all conscious memory is incomplete or even false, because it is always a selective reconstruction of a past event, the "memory" used by actors should be a specialized kind of fictive memory directed specifically toward the embodiment of a role, a focused "imagining" that activates selective visceral, sensorimotor, and semantic schemas. This focused use of memory has similarities to Strasberg's use of affective and sense memory, but with the crucial difference of making the (possibly merely) semantic shift from "remembering" or "recall" to "imagining." This can trigger a shift in the actor's relationship to, and thereby experience of, the memory. What matters most for the actor is not recapturing the most accurate memory (sensory or affective), but understanding that memory is a phenomenon of the moment, to be used in the service of creating and performing a role. Defining memory as a tool of the imagination, rather than the reproduction of something from the actor's literal history, liberates memory to be used more freely and theatrically. Memory becomes a re-imagining of some-thing that has cognitive, affective, and neurochemical utility, which is only provisionally or secondarily autobiographical or historically accurate. We no longer need to be concerned about reliving a past event as truthfully as possible, but can tap into memory as a tool to be used to make the present more alive, as part of the powers of imagination to make the actor's range of expression as wide and deep as possible. The science productively "de-objectifies" our relationship to experience; a character is no longer an entity to be accurately embodied, but a process to be explored and lived. It also "de-subjectifies" this relationship, through its organic perspective on the self. The self—our self—is no longer something that is fixed and set, but something which is a result of dynamic neurochemical processes that are always in flux and which it is possible to affect and change.

Imagination and image streams

Therefore: *Every movement you make on the stage, every word you speak, is the result of the right life of your imagination.*
(Stanislavsky 1936: 71)

We must have, first of all, an unbroken series of supposed circumstances in the midst of which our exercise is played. Secondly we must have a solid line of inner visions bound up with those circumstances, so that they will be *illustrated* for us. *During every moment we are on the stage, during every moment of the development of the action of the play, we must be aware either of the external circumstances which surround us (the whole material setting of the production), or of an inner chain of circumstances which we ourselves have imagined in order to illustrate our parts.*

Out of these moments will be formed an unbroken series of images, something like a moving picture [*kinolenta*]. As long as we are acting creatively, this film will unroll and be thrown on the screen of our inner vision, making vivid the circumstances among which we are moving. Moreover, these inner images create a corresponding mood, and arouse emotions, while holding us within the limits of the play.
(Stanislavsky 1936: 63–64, italics in the original)

The relationship between "fiction" and "reality" and between "feeling" and "reason" in the actor's process have been endlessly contested, beginning with Plato, continuing with Diderot, and going on till this day. For Stanislavsky and Strasberg, the focus was on engaging the actor "truthfully" with imaginary circumstances. In his chapter on "Action," the beginning of the discussion of technique in *An Actor Prepares*, Stanislavsky introduces the centrality of imagination, most powerfully through the discussion of "if": "[. . .] *if* acts as a lever to lift us out of the world of actuality into the realm of imagination" (Stanislavsky 1936: 46). For actors, image, imagery, and imagination are always key terms. While actors may initially deal with imagination and imagery at the level of semantic memory (facts, or consciously cognitive information, such as knowing July is winter in New Zealand), this is a preliminary stage of the actor's work, generally concerned with grasping technical aspects of a play's and production's material given circumstances. This analytical level of imagination, while necessary, is insufficient unless it is used as a springboard to inspire the actor's use or fabrication of episodic memory (personal experiences, "things that happened to you at a particular time and place," i.e., things experienced directly by the body, such as the taste of a fresh tomato).

Memories and imagination do not—indeed, cannot—exist without a foundational image of the body. Psychic images—whether they are of authentic past experiences or of an imagination of our self in fictive situations—are *always of the body*, since they are generated only within and by a body. Unconscious and conscious images of our bodies—both "remembered" and "imagined"—are the basis for how we negotiate our world. These images are how we learn and know how to drive a car, brush our teeth, make love, behave around our parents, behave around our enemies, behave around our friends, and how we project appropriate or useful ways to behave in new situations. The abstract question "How do you see yourself?" grows out of the primacy of the very specific image of our self as a body. Psychic images grow out of our body images or schemas, which are "the product (and producer) of the space between self and other, between sensations over time, between the inside and the outside, between and through bodily movements [. . .] a living, constantly developing organization of knowledge" (Wilson 1998: 173–174). (Here, "body image" means something quite different from what it means in the popular sense.) This view of various kinds of body images, fundamental components of our sense of self, manages to be simultaneously material and fluid, personal and social—like the best acting.

Damasio defines body images as mappings of body-states, which he connects with emotions and feelings by means of the somatic-marker hypothesis (Damasio 1999: 148). In Damasio's framework, there are two kinds of body images—from the body's interior, which provides information regarding our internal state, and from sensory probes such as the retina and cochlea, which provide information from the external environment (Damasio 1999: 195). These two sources provide an ongoing stream of foundational images in the mind that are "images of some kind of body event, [. . . their basis being] a collection of brain maps, that is, a collection of patterns of neuron activity and inactivity (neural patterns, for short) in a variety of sensory regions" (Damasio 1999: 197). These images, many of which are preconscious, are "brain constructions *prompted* by an object, rather than mirror reflections of the object" (Damasio 1999: 200). Just as a memory is never the same as the initial event that triggered it, the body image is not the same as the event triggering it, though, like memory, it is every bit as real in its own way and on its own terms. The body images:

> that flow in the mind are reflections of the interaction between the organism and the environment. [. . .] The mind exists for the body, is engaged in telling the story of the body's multifarious events, and uses that story to optimize the life of the organism.
> (Damasio 1999: 206)

In short, as Damasio so aptly puts it, the only reason mind exists is because there is a body to furnish it with contents—with images. Consciousness begins to arise when the flow of sensory images— the preconscious movie-in-the-brain about the states of the body —is accompanied by images of a self (Damasio 1999: 215). Here, the movie metaphor is a way of talking about the organism's engagement—first preconsciously—with the flow of bodily experiences that are "translated" into a conscious mental movie.

In his own way Stanislavsky understood the power of a flow of images and devised his own version of the movie-in-the-brain metaphor for the actor's use, as seen in the quotation that begins this section. Stanislavsky's moving picture is, at least implicitly, more about a personal or social narrative than a body-state one, which is where Damasio's begins. However, because there is no image without the body, Damasio's body-state movie is the only ground out of which any personal or psychological moving picture can grow. Regardless, Stanislavsky was adamant about the actor's need for a rigorous image-based score. (The relationship between body and imagination in performance has been studied at least as far back as Quintilian, the first century C.E. orator and rhetorician who described the power of *visiones,* sometimes drawn from painful personal experience, to inspire a speaker and thereby move his audience.)

Stanislavsky's imagination and "if" also relate to another cognitive neuroscience term: "as-if" body states. Research has shown that body-sensing areas of the brain reflect not only actual body states, but can also manufacture and deal with "false" ones (Damasio 1999: 118). These "as-if" body states can be thought of as imaginary ones that are essentially based on memory, i.e., recollections and reconstitutions of conscious and somatic experiences. Humans have some control over these as-if states. Because we can manipulate them to some degree for opportunistic ends, Stanislavsky's "if" taps into this aspect of how we function in order to activate the actor's imagination. The actor is constantly engaged in the manipulation of various kinds of body-states through the manipulation of imagination and environment, in order to embody certain conditions connected to playing a character. The use of "if" is also illuminated by other areas of research. Theory of Mind work by cognitive scientists such as Robert M. Gordon explores what we might call empathy or identification, our capacity to understand others—real or fictional—, by running cognitive simulations that allow us to pretend to be in their situation, in order to project their possible responses and actions. Similarly, research on mirror neurons is studying aspects of the neurological bases of these cognitive studies. The science is providing insight into this process commonly used by actors when creating a role.

Character and its relationship to given circumstances (the "facts" of a play and its situation) mirror the idea of a self or organism in relationship to an environment, while action can be aligned with the organism's attempts to interact successfully with the environment, based on the "movie-in-the-brain." Good actors tend to focus on images connected to episodic, rather than semantic, memory, for actors in the moment of performance are typically more concerned with personal experience, "things that happened to you at a particular time and place," things experienced by the body, i.e., facts or information more important for their emotional efficacy and power. When we create the right physical and imaginational environments, it produces an instrumental stream of images that result in the desired behavior and feeling. At bottom, all human beings rely on image-manipulation—a core element of the actor's work—to survive.

A note on "impulse"

One of the things that actors strive to do is to "act on impulse," a phrase referring to being able to respond spontaneously without censoring or constricting one's reaction. An actor who isn't "acting on impulse" is not present to the moment, including being present to her scene partner, and is limiting her responsiveness and imagination. But what is an impulse? The O.E.D. defines it as "Sudden or involuntary inclination or tendency to act, without premeditation or reflection," though, in relationship to acting, it is more useful to talk about freeness, responsiveness, and spontaneity—spontaneous in the sense "Of personal actions: Arising or proceeding entirely from natural impulse, without any external stimulus or constraint; voluntary and of its own accord." When we speak of an actor's ability to act on impulses in performance, we are necessarily invoking the paradoxical nature of spontaneity in the actor's process, for "the actor's spontaneous vitality seems to depend on the extent to which his actions and thoughts have been automatized, made second nature" (Roach 1993: 16). The successful spontaneous response in the moment depends upon the actor's rehearsal and repetition of an effective performance score, i.e., a score made spontaneous through successful habituation. The actor is spontaneous both in the sense of being habituated and in the sense of being immediate and vital—able to "act on impulse."

An actor having difficulty acting on impulse, whether in rehearsal or performance, may be making one of the following missteps: (1) she is acting with insufficient information, e.g., she doesn't have a handle on given circumstances, beginning with a strong grasp of the semantic or cultural information in or supporting the text, or hasn't done sufficient preparation; (2) she is using the wrong point of attention or focus, i.e., she has misdefined the problem or the objective (this can be due to shortfalls in number 1); (3) she misunderstands the relationship between emotion/feeling and action, e.g., she is focused on a state or a feeling, rather than a task or situation (this is a corollary to number 2); (4) she is limiting or constraining her imagination; (5) she is suspicious of genuine theatricality and energy, sometimes inappropriately conflating thoughtfulness or tension with emotional authenticity, because a large, unexpected, or nonstereotypical response can't be an "authentic" one (the cursed legacy of some film and TV acting); or (6) she is afraid of failing or of looking foolish. The bottom line is that acting on impulse is best supported within a highly specific context, shaped through a vivid engagement with given circumstances and the development of a meticulous physical and mental score that allows the actor to respond to the immediate presence of her partner rather than, e.g., the reality of the immediate presence of everyone else in the room, whether it be teacher, director, or audience.

Towards application

Using the findings of science can move us past some historical and cultural conventions, as well as habits of thought, that are counterproductive for actors. All actors don't need to know a great deal about cognitive neuroscience. However, there is evidence that we need to reframe our sense of self and "emotional truth," not to mention theatricality, in light of a more nuanced and specific grasp of the interrelationship among the physical, the emotional, and the consciously cognitive. In particular, it is time to redefine our sense of action and image/ination by divorcing it from vocabularies of twentieth-century psychology and cultural production that have limited our capacity for exploring and embodying theatrical material. The science provides a way of acknowledging and using for our benefit the contingency and fluidity of experience and consciousness.

Operating from the provisional biological and cultural perspective I've been describing, the actor can more consciously and productively create a reliable score for a performance. Two basic applications could be in how we might emphasize episodic, rather than rely on semantic, memory, and in how we reinforce neural patterns and responses that break free of culturally and personally habituated framings of the "problem" of the character. This provides a guide for actors to create more consciously a vivid and living string of both cascading and anchoring images that draw on sensory, affective, and explicit memory, and to connect this to a detailed kinesthetic score that supports the body-mapping of those images. The applications of this research must be as varied as the artists employing them, for this work, like Stanislavsky's, is not about a cookbook formula but about basic principles. The point is to find strategies and ways of working as actors for maximum *act*-ivation. As with other approaches, the ultimate goal is to discover and define given circumstances to create a vital sense of unfolding embodiment, regardless of the particular piece.

This work also requires that we redefine our relationship to certain psychophysical experiences, for sometimes what may typically be seen as an emotional or psychological issue in acting is actually, on a deeper level, better understood as a physical, or body-state, issue. As actors and human beings, we are habituated—literally, creatures of habit—when it comes to interpreting homeostatic and autonomic symptoms that rise to the level of consciousness. We register body-states—heart-rate, respiration, muscle tension, temperature, etc.—and interpret them as positive or negative in such a way that, e.g., the same state could be interpreted as either excitement or anxiety, depending on the individual and her history and proclivities. The issue is how emotions surface as feelings, which we then translate into language. Often, the "mistranslation" of somatic and sensory representations at the semantic or cultural or pseudo-psychotherapeutic level has led to a great deal of boring, self-conscious acting, which can have to do with the actor's exertion of trying to "live the role" or "become the character" within a narrow range of personal or cultural "authenticity." Narrowness was never Stanislavsky's goal: he worked with Shakespeare, Molière, and Mozart, as well as Chekhov and Gorky. I am reminded again of the mistranslation of Stanislavsky's key term, *perezhivanie*, which is literally "living *through*," not "living," the role; the actor does not become the character, but experiences or lives life *through* the character as she performs a meticulously shaped score.

Perhaps one of the most valuable aspects of this application is that it gives us the knowledge to say goodbye to Descartes' body–mind split definitively and to take the next step in demystifying Diderot's paradox. It moves us beyond the tired old arguments about how "split" or how "merged" actor and role are, and whose feelings are being experienced or witnessed at any given moment —the actor's or the character's—, not to mention how "truthful" or "believable" that expression is. A new vocabulary based on neurocognitive research provides a specific, material way of talking about the phenomenon of acting rather as that of a single organism, keeping the psychoanalytic or psychological in its proper and useful place. "Taking on a character" or "imbibing the reality" of a role become recontextualized as strategies about *performance*, because the character becomes a set of choices and behaviors—a process, rather than a discrete entity, a motivated movement, rather than a gloss of feeling—, supported by what the actor brings to the role. That is, a character becomes a dance performed by the only discrete entity there is—the actor. There is no character in any fixed or pre-set sense; as in life, there is only the progress of a particular individual moving through a particular context, changing with each moment. What the actor is doing becomes simply—and complexly —that: what the *actor* is *doing*.

Chapter 4

Applications

What follows are actual and theoretical applications of this work. All of the cases are about traditionally scripted theatre, rather than improvisational or experimental performance; however, since all performance is ultimately about how images in somebody's head work on the bodies of the performer and of the audience, I believe there can be applications for any kind of theatre (but that is another book). Here, the emphasis is on the embodiment of text. In the examples I discuss, the actor's goal is to develop a compelling performance by making specific and charged choices through engaging image, language, and action in ways that are integrated with and support those of their fellow performers. It is all about the "who," "where," "when," "what," "why," and language of the play and its interface with particular actors, particular idiosyncratic individuals.

The process I describe is typically one of initial careful reading—even excavation—of the text, finding the most personal connections with it, and then constant "re-reading" through embodiment and enactment, repetition, refinement, and filling in the life lived in the performance. One of its foundations is the paradox that the more thoroughly automatic or patterned a performance is—or spontaneous, in biological terms—, the freer the actor is to respond spontaneously, in intuitive and creative terms, in the moment.

The projects I will be considering are Shakespeare's *Hamlet*, Rebecca Gilman's *Boy Gets Girl*, Suzan-Lori Parks' *Venus*, Anton Chekhov's *Three Sisters*, and a colleague's application of elements of this research in his classes and in directing Timberlake Wertenbaker's *Our Country's Good*. The discussion of Shakespeare focuses on a hypothetical exercise directed toward engaging the "To be or not to be" soliloquy. The next three are case studies of scripts I have directed; these provide examples of how I used this research with contemporary US realism, contemporary US expressionism (for want of a better way of describing Parks' fascinating play), and Chekov.

Exercise: *Hamlet*

To be, or not to be, that is the question:
Whether 'tis nobler in the mind to suffer
The slings and arrows of outrageous fortune
Or to take arms against a sea of troubles,
And by opposing end them. To die—to sleep—
No more; and by a sleep to say we end
The heartache, and the thousand natural shocks
That flesh is heir to. 'Tis a consummation
Devoutly to be wished. To die—to sleep,
To sleep—perchance to dream: ay, there's the rub!
For in that sleep of death what dreams may come
When we have shuffled off this mortal coil,
Must give us pause. There's the respect
That makes calamity of so long life,
For who would bear the whips and scorns of time,
The oppressor's wrong, the proud man's contumely,
The pangs of despised love, the law's delay,
The insolence of office, and the spurns
That patient merit of the unworthy takes
When he himself might his quietus make
With a bare bodkin? Who would these fardels bear,
To grunt and sweat under a weary life,
But that the dread of something after death—
The undiscovered country, from whose bourn
No traveller returns—puzzles the will,
And makes us rather bear those ills we have
Than fly to others that we know not of?
Thus conscience doth make cowards of us all,
And thus the native hue of resolution
Is sicklied o'er with the pale cast of thought,
And enterprises of great pith and moment
With this regard their currents turn awry

And lose the name of action.—Soft you now!
The fair Ophelia. Nymph, in thy orisons
Be all my sins remember'd.

(Shakespeare, *Hamlet* III, i, 64–98)

I'm standing off-stage, preparing to enter for Act III, scene i of *Hamlet*.

I enter to do the "To be or not to be" soliloquy.

I'm coming from the battlements and it's sunny / rainy / hot / cold; it's November / April / August; I'm coming from the dungeon / kitchen / bedroom; I haven't slept / just woke up / and it's midday / evening / morning.

I'm hungry / sated / thirsty. I have / don't have a headache.

I'm passing through on my way to throw myself off the battlements and kill myself / I'm trying to decide if I should take action about my father's death and, if so, what kind / I'm trying to decide if I should kill myself instead / I'm looking for Ophelia / I'm looking for a priest.

As I enter I feel as though I'm crawling / flying / sliding / scratching / pressing / slashing / pushing / fidgeting / on speed / Quaaludes / LSD / whiskey.

The audience is: an ally / an enemy / they want to kill me / they want to comfort me / they're my good elder / my peer / my therapist / my best friend / my father / they're utter strangers. They look funny, scary, absurd, wise, compassionate. (How can you use what you actually feel from the audience, incorporating it into your work?)

I want them to embrace me passionately / hold me tenderly / sit quietly with me / put their hand on my brow / put their hand on my heart / put me out of my misery.

Say, "To be or not to be, that is the question."

Say, "To live or not to live, that is the issue."

Say, "Should I take action or not, that's what I have to decide."

Say, "Should I kill myself or not, that's what I'm trying to decide."

Say, "Not to be or to be, that is the problem."

Again, say, "To be or not to be, that is the question."

Contemplate the differences—in terms of the associations and images evoked, in terms of the feeling in the mouth, in terms of the rhythms of the phrase.

What is the image in your head at the moment of speaking "to be"? "not to be"? What does your "not being" look/feel like?

What do you see when you see slings? Arrows? From where are they coming?

What's the feeling behind outrageous? How outrageous? What are your personal associations with "outrage"—anger / revulsion / fear / violation / rage / irony and absurdity? What are Hamlet's associations, as you understand them? Is there a connection to be made?

What kind of arms? What do they look like? What do they feel like in your hands? Are you talking about a rapier? A broadsword? A dagger? An Uzi? Have you ever held or used any of these weapons?

What kind of sea? What does this sea of troubles look like? What, personally, has been your experience of the sea? What kind of troubles? What does this feel like visually, aurally, kinesthetically? What would it feel like to end them?

"To die"—is this a repetition of "to take arms" or is it a next step / a discovery / a realization / a hope / a fear?

What image or impulse toggles you over from "die" to "sleep"? Where is it located in your body? In your heart? In your belly?

What does your heartache feel like? Where specifically is it in your body?

What do you feel / see when you say "natural shocks"? What do you want the audience to feel / see?

What do the sounds—"THouSand naCHural SHockS that fleSH iS heir to. 'TiS a conSummaSHion devoutly to be wiSHed"—do to you? What do you want the sounds to do to the audience?

What is the toggle from "sleep" to "dream"? Where does "dream" arise from in your body: your head? your heart? your solar plexus? your belly?

Have you ever been whipped or lashed? Scorned?

When you say "bare bodkin," do you mean a "mere bodkin" or an "unsheathed bodkin"? What does your bodkin look like? Do you have the bodkin on you? Do you show it to the audience?

What on earth is a fardle? I mean, what does it look like? How much does it weigh? What does it feel like to bear one?

"The dread of something after death"—what images are in your head? Which are Hamlet's? Which are yours? Is there an overlap? What scares the crap out of you? Can you use this? What are you / what is Hamlet afraid to discover in the undiscovered country?

What is the hue of your resolution—hot white? blue? red? black? What is the color of your pale cast of thought—green? blue? yellow?

When you see Ophelia, does it hit you in the heart? the solar plexus? the face? the belly? the groin? Where do you feel the impact?

A nymph is a beautiful demigoddess who lives in places of great natural beauty. But did Shakespeare/does Hamlet know that "nymph" is related to "nympha," a word for the labia minora? What might this do to how you experience "in thy orisons be all my sins remember'd," in terms of the fraught sexuality of the relationship between Hamlet and Ophelia? What are the sins to which Hamlet refers? Are they connected to his relationship with Ophelia? are they sexual? emotional? both? What do they look / smell / feel like in the moment of speaking? What specifically is Hamlet / are you feeling in your body when you choose the word "sins"?

The entire play could, and probably should, be treated with this kind of care and attention as a means of unlocking the actor's psychophysical being. The goal is to develop a detailed score, a stream of images—which, of course, can and will be adjusted as the process continues—that puts the play into the actor's body as vividly and immediately as possible. A good number of the preceding questions on the soliloquy are the kind that an actor might often ask while preparing the piece, but I would argue that the intense detail and the nature of some of the questions, e.g., such as where the body-toggle from "sleep" to "dream" is, and what the color of the hue of resolution is, are not typical, as is the relative lack of concern in this phase of the work for Hamlet's "psychology" or motive and the intense focus on images that come from or reside in the body. This is not an intellectual or dramaturgical exercise. It is about waking up the body by going through the mind (or, as Stanislavsky might put it, constructing a detailed filmstrip to reach the unconscious by conscious means . . .).

Case study: Rebecca Gilman's *Boy Gets Girl*

I was invited by Dallas's Echo Theatre, a small professional theatre that produces scripts by women and focuses on quality in casting and acting, to direct Rebecca Gilman's *Boy Gets Girl* in spring 2003. The script tells the story of Theresa Bedell, a writer for a popular magazine, who is terrorized by a seemingly charming blind date who turns out to be an increasingly threatening stalker. Our production of the seven-character play, which has two acts in eighteen scenes, had the standard three-week, three-hour a day rehearsal period, and was presented in a small, roughly 100-seat house. The multiple settings include Theresa's office at the magazine, the reception office, her apartment, a couple of restaurants, a pornography filmmaker's office, and a hospital room. Rapid scene

changes compel the actors (especially one playing the central character, who is in all but one of the scenes and has a costume change
for each one) to shift gears quickly from scene to scene. Besides the
particular challenges presented by this script, we were an eclectic
group, with actors who had very little experience or training to
those who had a great deal; all came out of professional, rather
than academic training, backgrounds. I had known the leading
actor, Ellen Locy, prior to auditions, but none of the others, though
I had seen the work of two; I had directed none of them before.

Plot is central to this piece—particularly in the sense of a classic-
ally melodramatic "What's going to happen to Theresa?"—, but
it's straightforward (in the sense of Aristotle's simple plot structure),
so focusing just on plot isn't enough for a successful production.
Rather, success depends on marrying the suspense of the piece to
richly-embodied characters with nuanced relationships that develop
over the course of the evening. The straightforward nature of the
script is a blessing, because the narrative is accessible and familiar,
and a curse, for it makes it easier to remain formulaic in playing
clichés of realism rather than explore the play's action and unfolding
relationships more genuinely. I began our rehearsals as most do,
laying out the general direction for the play and the nature and tone
of its world. We then began looking at the accumulating movement
in each scene and how these were connected to the movement of
the play as a whole, particularly in terms of the growing threat
facing Theresa and how this affected the various relationships.
Perhaps what is different from some others' processes is that I
required the actors to treat the text "like Shakespeare, even though
it isn't Shakespeare," i.e., I challenged them to be word-perfect in
memorizing and working with the play's language. This was
necessary in order for them to be able to work as specifically and
personally as possible in selecting and constructing images to carry
them through the action. Clarity of language is crucial, for it is a
direct reflection of clarity in relationship to image and action. If the
language changes or is unclear, then the image changes or is unclear;
and this manifests itself in changes or lack of clarity in the action,
which is an outgrowth of and response to imagination. (I'm speaking
about most traditional, text-based theatre, and not so much about
improvisational or interactive performances.) As with any rehearsal
process, we made many amendments and changes along the way,
increasingly refining the piece. But I was specifically challenging the
actors to have a specific stream of sensory and kinesthetic images

to carry them through each scene, as well as specific images in mind prior to entering for any scene. A few of the actors were more used to being more "personal" or intuitive (or I might say casual) in their approach to rehearsal, but overall the more technical approach led to some success (three of the seven actors were nominated for "best actor" in their categories in Dallas's major theatre awards event, and one of them won).

When I spoke with Ellen after the show had closed about what her experience had been, she confirmed what I had thought was true about my observations of her process. For her, the big difference in the work we had done was the degree to which she had to be specific in approaching this conventionally realistic, seemingly simple text—word by word, image by image. She described how this process became "deeper and fuller and richer" for her over the course of rehearsals and the three-week run of the show as the stream and cascade of images in her mind increasingly filled up and in fact drove the action. As the work progressed, Ellen increasingly felt the need to see or at least engage in some sensory way absolutely everything she was talking about. This meant getting personally specific with images (visual, aural, experiential, etc.) about things she talked about, even in passing, ranging from Kuala Lumpur to sandwiches to William Dean Howells to Terre Haute; this required library and internet research, and also watching made-for-TV stalker movies and a bit of soft porn, since one of the characters is a Russ Meyer type. It meant developing a consciously vivid visual and kinesthetic sense for the layout of the offices outside of her office door. Besides this, her construction of personal images of Theresa Bedell's reported experiences—the explicit memory of the character—, based on information in the script, was crucial to activating and driving her interactions with the other characters; these character-memory images, an updated and recontextualized version of sense and affective memory, provided color and urgency to her engaging her fellow actors.

Ellen summed up as follows, from her perspective as a TV/film/commercial/stage actress who comes out of nonacademic training grounded in Strasberg-based psychological realism. The key to success was being sure each referent had personal meaning for her as an actor/character, in order for her to anchor the referent and action of the moment and to drive it into the next moment. Perhaps one of the most interesting things that occurred was that Ellen's work with images regularly led her to very unexpected line readings, because the conscious specificity of the image took her away from pedestrian and mundane interpretations; it prevented her from glossing over text and falling back on less than fully conscious readings based on choices habituated through her past experiences. This approach also meant that Ellen was responding more immediately to what she was receiving from her scene partners, for she was developing a corollary pattern of focusing on their words and behaviors as specifically as she was engaging her own. In our conversation Ellen wrapped up by saying, "The specific images in your head open you up to more possibilities to what can be happening in a scene or a performance, into the unexpected, because it comes from a very personal engagement with the script" (Locy 2003). From Ellen's perspective it could be argued that the process was essentially a rich integration of her Strasberg-influenced background with Shakespeare-influenced close readings, and it wouldn't be necessary—or even fruitful—to disagree with this in terms of her application of technique. This approach would serve any of the best modern playwrights, such as Samuel Beckett, Harold Pinter, and David Mamet, who craft "mundane" language so that it is in fact more like poetry than conventional prose, especially in its ability to provide a powerful rhythmic and imagistic impetus for the actor's embodiment; the feeling and discovery come fully only with the actor's rigorous engagement with the words and punctuation as written on the page. The same should be true for the actor's work on almost any well-written modern play, including *Boy Gets Girl*.

During rehearsals I didn't discuss the principles of cognitive neuroscience with Ellen, or how they were influencing my direction and coaching. For one thing, I was in a very preliminary phase of my research. More importantly, three weeks of rehearsal for about eighteen hours a week meant we needed to work very quickly and pragmatically. However, I am sure my work with her would not have been as rigorous without the insight I was gleaning from my research. What in fact I was doing through much of the rehearsal process was guiding Ellen to create a very detailed stream of mental images, connected to the script and to her fellow actors, so that as many moments as possible were not just about "telling," but about feeling, in the sense of being present to the character's story and immediate world in respect to both the senses and affect. What follows is one of Theresa's speeches from *Boy Gets Girl* and a description of how we approached constructing an image stream:

Okay. When I was a freshman in college, I dated a guy who was a bartender. I would go and sit at the bar and wait for him to get off work. And there was this old man there who was always drinking alone and I always felt sorry for him. One night, he started talking to me, telling me all about his life and how he had lost his wife and how his children didn't speak to him anymore, and I felt really sorry for him and I told him I felt bad for him and he told me it would make him feel better to kiss a pretty girl. So I let him kiss me. On the mouth. *(Beat.)* I didn't want to at all. He was an old drunk and it made me sick. But I did it anyway because it's what I thought I was supposed to do. I was supposed to be nice.

(Gilman 2002: 85)

In this speech from Act II, scene iii, Theresa is trying to figure out why she is overly nice and compliant, rather than honest and self-respecting, in situations with men. If the actor were working with an approach typical of American psychological realism, she might create a general imaginary memory and feeling about this narrative, sometimes as part of a detailed character biography or back story that the actor could develop far beyond the information and even the events contained in the script. This could also use Strasberg's technique of substitution to connect the story to elements of the actor's personal life. This approach can work, but it sometimes leads the actor to focus on a feeling *about* what they are doing rather than on feeling *what* they are doing. These two things are radically different: a feeling about a scene is not the same thing as being in the scene. Another way to describe this is that the actor can be busier feeling the (character's or her own) feelings than being present to the feeling that arises in the moment of the acting.

In our approach, Theresa's speech, a response to a story just told by another character, is an attempt to understand the other character's opinion that, when we find ourselves in bad or dangerous situations, "we can't always tell how much is us and how much is the world around us" (Gilman 2002: 84). Hearing this, Theresa is immediately reminded of her freshman year in college and an incident she hasn't thought of in two decades, as far as we know; this in itself indicates that it has weight or emotional "charge" for the character in this moment. The images evoked by the speech include herself as a freshman (the actor would possibly visualize or "re-member" clothing, hair, sensory specifics related to the bartender boyfriend, vulnerability), the bar (where she sat, how long she'd been waiting and what it felt like, where the old man sat, time of year, time of night, the smell, the crowd or lack of it, how much she had to drink), the old man (hair, skin, clothing, smell, hands, face, voice), the feeling of the kiss (his mouth, along with all the preceding). These images are just a few of the many that could be used, drawn directly from the particular event Theresa describes in this brief speech, and which have no need of embellishment in further biography or back-story. They are vivid enough on their own, for the purpose of vitality in the moment, honing on the physical as well as the emotional feeling of the intrusive interchange between the girl and the old man, and then on Theresa's realization of her participation in her own violation.

Cues for the physical, and hence psychic, feeling of the movement of the language are also provided by the language's punctuation. The one-word sentence, "Okay," is followed by a full stop, which is then followed by two brief, descriptive sentences; these are a set-up for Theresa to share something difficult, or perhaps to reconstruct things in her head. A very long sentence follows; it begins with "One night" and is broken only by two commas before ending with "pretty girl"; I feel rushed and a bit out of control when I read this sentence straight through without stopping or taking a significant breath. Again, the important thing here is how Theresa feels in the present, not the information of the man's story. Further, based on the sentence's structure the problem is also not a struggle on Theresa's part to remember or to reconnect with this past moment; the punctuation clearly indicates that she is remembering things easily and fluidly. What matters is the onrush of feeling Theresa has as she recollects the event, e.g., the way he sounded, looked, and smelled when he said "kiss a pretty girl." The impact for the actor (and the audience as well, based on research on mirror and simulation neuronal systems) on "So I let him kiss me. On the mouth" is dependent on the actor having very specific kinesthetic and olfactory images—of the old man's smells, lips, the feeling on her mouth, her nausea and physical revulsion—and of Theresa's reaction to this in the moment of remembering. If the image score is effective, the "*Beat*" will happen organically; without the construction of a highly personal, episodic memory of the violating kiss, the informational, semantic memory of the story will be dramatically incomplete. The "*Beat*" is followed by four declarative sentences, all composed of mostly one-syllable words, each about some aspect of what Theresa felt at that moment when she was a freshman and let the old man kiss her.

The issue becomes, how does the actor structure Theresa's feelings in the now as she recounts her feelings of the past? Questions related to these lines might have to do with whether Theresa has thought through these responses before: is this something she is realizing only as she speaks? What is the feeling for her in the moment of "I didn't want to at all"? How strong is this, what color or texture? What kind of sick, not just back then, but what is the feeling of the sick in the now? Ellen and I worked on this by referring back to the purpose, the action, that initiated the speech—to begin to figure out how Theresa might be complicit in her bad situation and to begin to find a way to change this. Ellen used a situation, a moment, from her own life when she had been "nice" and it had cost her, and used it to trigger a connection to Theresa's "nice." The actor does not "play" her past or these choices, but merely reacts to the stream of images she has set up as they arise. In this regard the work is different from Strasberg's psychological, even psychoanalytic, approach to substitution. The images do not need to make "logical" (i.e., rational or reasonable) or even "biographical" sense, any more than the images that pass through our heads at any given moment of the day make sense. They need only follow an artistic logic that serves the particular actor. They need to have psychophysical *efficacy* in engaging the actor, and thereby moving the audience. This approach is a descendent of Stanislavsky's method of active analysis, in that it is focused on devising a detailed performance score, a "filmstrip" in the mind.

Case study: Suzan-Lori Parks' *Venus*

I directed *Venus* in fall 2002 with BFA (junior and senior) and MFA students in Southern Methodist University's theatre season as a workshop production, focused on acting. It was an opportunity for our students to engage material by a leading contemporary playwright and to work in a very particular style and mode. I had a prior relationship as a teacher with almost all the cast, which provided us with some shared history and vocabulary; having this common ground from the start meant that we could jump into the heart of the play more quickly. Like most of Parks' plays, *Venus* on the page is structured almost more like music, poetry, or architecture than like a conventional drama. It has Parks' standard use of "rests" and "spells," as well as idiosyncratic spellings and punctuation (or lack of them); the play's thirty-one scenes are numbered like a countdown, and, within the frame of a carnival sideshow, run in chronological order from Sartje Baartman's departure for Europe to her death. Because of the challenging orthography of the script, we treated the first phase of rehearsal explicitly like an archaeological dig, "excavating" the themes and narrative of the play. These are straightforward, if one looks at the given circumstances and motifs embodied in the pages' concrete poetry; there is a well-developed story with carefully emotionally defined relationships among the main characters, centered on Sartje's desire for success, acceptance, and, most importantly, love, and how she is abused by those with power over her, culminating with her betrayal by the Baron Docteur. The work of the production in general was to guide the actors to create very clear mental images for themselves that they could use to create vivid physical images in telling the story for the audience. Ours was a minimally produced piece; we had rehearsal clothes, some hand props, a few small modular set pieces, Sartje's cage/cell, her bodysuit, and lighting, but not much more, and all sound cues were live. Because of this spareness, it was particularly important that the images and story be vivid for the actors, since they had to tell a story, set in a kind of early nineteenth century that starts in a kind of southern Africa and moves to a kind of England and France, that could move the audience without much in the way of formal design elements. To aid this we used accents for the various characters, which is not required (and some could argue is counter-indicated by the script, because of Parks' orthography); however, this helped the actors distinguish more effectively among the different characters they were playing (e.g., the actress playing the Grade-School Chum also played the South African Man's Brother and the English Mother Showman, while the chorus members played English sideshow freaks, gawkers, jurists, and French anatomists) and helped the audience with the play's movement amongst its fictional locations. The specific sounds also fostered certain kinds of images and suppressed others.

One scene in which image and action developed in ways I could not have anticipated was in the latter half of Scene 9, "Her Charming Hands / An Anatomical Columbus." The way this scene between the Baron Docteur and the Grade-School Chum eventually ended up being approached and staged was an explicit example of how image and embodiment tested and proved the research in cognitive neuroscience that I had been doing. The text is:

> (The Grade-School Chum appears as if out of thin air.)
> THE GRADE-SCHOOL CHUM.
> THE BARON DOCTEUR.
>
> THE GRADE-SCHOOL CHUM.
> THE BARON DOCTEUR.
>
> THE GRADE-SCHOOL CHUM.
> The door was wide open.
> I walked right in.
> You 2 should keep yr voices down.
> Everyone kin hear yr business.
> *(Rest.)*
> Don't you recognize me?
>
> THE BARON DOCTEUR.
> Can't say I do.
>
> THE GRADE-SCHOOL CHUM.
> We went to school together.
> Remember?
> *(Rest.)*
>
> THE BARON DOCTEUR.
>
> THE GRADE-SCHOOL CHUM.
> *(Rest.)*
>
> THE BARON DOCTEUR.
> Vaguely.
>
> THE GRADE-SCHOOL CHUM.
> I was the one who ripped the wings off the flies.
> We were like brothers.
> Hug me!

THE BARON DOCTEUR.
Beat it.

THE GRADE-SCHOOL CHUM.
Whats that thing around yr neck?

THE BARON DOCTEUR.
None of yr business.

THE GRADE-SCHOOL CHUM.
Get rid of her.
Shes not yr type.

THE BARON DOCTEUR.
Good evening, Sir.
I'll show you out.

THE GRADE-SCHOOL CHUM.
Yr wifes distraught.

THE BARON DOCTEUR.
No she is not!

THE GRADE-SCHOOL CHUM.
Yr reputation is in shambles.

THE BARON DOCTEUR.
My discoveriesll right that.

THE GRADE-SCHOOL CHUM.
You better publish those discoveries soon, Old Friend,
The Academy won't wait forever.

THE BARON DOCTEUR.
I'll dissect her soon enough!

THE GRADE-SCHOOL CHUM.
I've come as a friend.
Giving friendly advice.

THE BARON DOCTEUR.
Friend.
To her I am a mere
Anatomical Columbus.
Lemme read you a little
of what Ive written so far.
Where to begin? *Uh hehm.*
(He reads from his notebook.)
(("... the vast protuberance of her buttocks ...
the somewhat brutish appearance of her face."))

THE GRADE-SCHOOL CHUM.
So, get rid of her!
Break with her!
Kick her out on her fat ass!

THE BARON DOCTEUR.
But, I
I love her.
I love her!!

(Parks 1998: 131–133)

The Grade-School Chum's goal, as it always is, is to persuade the Baron to abandon the Venus. The Grade-School Chum has no interaction with any character but the Baron, and therefore can be seen as existing on a different level than all the other characters, who freely interact with each other. This meant that we could view the Grade-School Chum as something "other," e.g., the devil, a projection of the Baron's darker self, the embodiment of all things bad about post-Enlightenment sensibilities, which greatly expanded the possibilities for interpretation of what was going on with this character and what it meant for the Baron Docteur in his struggle. Removing the Grade-School Chum from the "realistic" and even the "human" allowed us to work metaphorically, in terms of images and dream, rather than in terms of conventional psychological realism. The two actors (the Baron Docteur played by an MFA man, the Grade-School Chum played by a BFA woman, following the cross-gender casting of earlier productions) viewed the task of their characters in this scene as a negotiation, a dance of resistance and desire growing out of the conflict between the Baron Docteur's love for Sartje and his racism and drive to use his "Venus" to fulfill his scientific ambitions. The image of a dance became serendipitous: we had the potential for some accompaniment, since the actor playing the Negro Resurrectionist was using an African drum to punctuate moments and provide rhythmic drive for the play, and I had already asked the cast to think about how the drum might be employed to support the story. Out of this came the actors' idea to try playing the scene as a tango. They worked with our movement teacher Sara Romersberger to devise a detailed physical score that we then revised in only minor ways before inserting it into the show. Following an initial pass of the characters around each other, the dance began with the Grade-School Chum's command, "Hug me!," and then built in increasing pressure, with the characters repeatedly breaking apart and coming together, until "*I love her!!*"

The tango worked as performance for the audience, because it theatrically embodied the scene's story—both dark and absurd; the dance both brought to life the Grade-School Chum's seduction of the Baron Docteur to abandon the Venus, and provided a charged and appropriately disorienting musical interlude (no doubt enhanced by the fact that a man and woman with strong French accents were playing the two male characters). It also worked for the actors, for it was an anchoring, literally step-by-step psychophysicalization of the action—a kind of hyper-choreography whose primary purpose was to provide a sequence of embodied images to move forward the emotional, intellectual, and even erotic struggle between and within the characters. The steps in this process were (1) laying a foundation with the themes, basic narrative, and character given circumstances of the script, (2) defining the basic/central action of the scene itself, and (3) drawing out specific images and givens of our company and the moment-by-moment of the text. Because the Baron and the Grade-School Chum were played with French accents, this may well have led the actors to the image of a (Continental, or at least exotic) tango on some level. Our framework provided both personal autonomy and textual specificity in "image manufacturing."

Case study: Anton Chekhov's *Three Sisters*

In fall 2005 I directed Chekhov's *Three Sisters* with a cast of four third-year MFA students and ten BFA students. Based on the principles I've been discussing in this book, at the beginning of the process I was particularly attentive to providing not only general semantic information, e.g., background on Chekhov, Russia at the turn of the twentieth century, but also paid close attention to working with the actors "non-semantically" by working on their bodies, through their eyes, their ears, and in space.

At the beginning I provided pictures of the play's world by showing the cast dozens of pictures related to that world: realist and impressionist Russian paintings of the period, photographs of the Russian countryside, homes, and forests in all seasons, and I also paid particular attention to photographs of the military. I believe it may have been significant that I presented these images in very large format on black background in PowerPoint so that they would have a great impact on the actor's visual field (an 8′ × 8′ image of a birch forest in early September or a muddy, rutted, snowy provincial road in May is more striking than a 8″ × 8″ one). These visual images provided a virtual substitute for actual experiences of the characters. I incorporated music and sound as much as possible into the process, including all music called for in the text; we were fortunate to have a skilled pianist in the part of Tuzenbach to play Tchaikovsky, Chopin, and folk music, and another cast member could play violin off-stage for Andrei. This enriched aural environment significantly guided the rhythms of the play. One early rehearsal took the actors playing military characters through a "boot camp" experience to whet their imaginations by giving them a taste of the "real thing"; it was led by a cast member who had been a student in the Air Force Academy years ago (ironically, the actor playing Chebutykin, the least military of the military men).

Other early rehearsals were devoted to improvisations to clarify each cast member's relationships with every other character in the play. One exercise involved the actors, one at a time, silently arranging the company, including themselves, in a three-dimensional sculpture that embodied the interpersonal world of the play from that particular character's perspective; for example, many actors placed the three sisters in the center of the room or sometimes on a platform, while Natasha and Solyony often found themselves off in a corner (and in one case out the door). A number of the cast remarked that the exercise gave them a vivid sense of how the others saw their characters, but, perhaps more interestingly, it gave them a physical and visual experience of where they weren't clear about a relationship and needed to do some more work. This is important for all plays, but particularly so for Chekhov and *Three Sisters*, in which all of the characters know each other and simultaneously inhabit the same space. The idea for this exercise was directly inspired by Lakoff and Johnson's discussions of how the experience of our bodies provides us with the vocabularies and images for how we see and experience the world.

After the production closed, I asked David Matherly, the senior who played Tuzenbach, if he would read some excerpts from the book manuscript and then talk with me about how it resonated with his work, if at all, and how it might be pertinent to his acting. He was particularly thoughtful in his engagement, and even raised some points that hadn't occurred to me. From his perspective, semantic memory was as important as episodic memory, for the former provides a foundation for the latter in his process. He specifically described how learning facts about Russia was a crucial precursor for his understanding and personalizing Tuzenbach's world. As he put it, "Semantic memory allows me to engage my imagination in regard to things I haven't experienced. So I guess I create my own imaginary episodic memory." (David also discussed the importance of semantic information in regard to the mechanics and analysis of Shakespeare, on which he was working in class at the same time.) Following his development of a sufficient store of "semantic" information for Tuzenbach, an important part of not only David's memorization of lines, but also owning of the part, was his immersion in extensive repetition of lines; this allowed him to refine his images, and thereby make more specific the feelings that eventually attached to the words.

He was also thoughtful about how his process was affected by work with a scene partner: "I set the images initially, but they change depending on the other actors or the performance." For David, the preparatory work is its own "place marker"—a base line to which he could return when needed. David observed that, just as the self is a process, so is the actor's use of images. For him, these are initially set to a greater or lesser degree, but are in flux once he gets into rehearsal with another actor or into perform-ance. In describing his experience in *Three Sisters*, he said, "I was constantly revising the work, based on the process." He became particularly aware that, during the Act I scene between Tuzenbach and Irina, he was remaining open enough to his partner to allow the images to change based on what he was receiving from her. David described his overall process, in terms of each of the phases, as being the most detailed, meticulous image work he has done, even much more than his experience of traditional moment-to-moment work. He compared it to the work of a dancer, who can change the feeling of a moment substantially by making the smallest change, even "just bending a finger—the whole feeling changes."

Conversations with a master acting teacher

The head of our Acting programs, Michael Connolly, is a Stanislavsky-based professional actor, a member of the Utah Shakespearean Festival company, a director, and a superb acting teacher and coach. He works primarily with classic texts of the Western canon, especially Shakespeare. In his teaching and coaching, Michael's central concern is to guide the actor to be emotionally full, intellectually specific, and physically compelling (Connolly 2003). He is interested in the applications of neurocognitive research to acting because it acknowledges how we actually function in the world; it links psychology and biology, describing how aspects of the actor's being are integrated. It also provides support for questioning twentieth-century approaches that compartmentalize different aspects of the actor's being, whether it be separating acting from voice, voice from movement, or all of this from critical thinking and analysis. He believes this approach refigures the sequence of events that leads to the embodiment of research, text work, personal history, and analysis in the service of performance. Michael and I have both found that this approach frees us from conventional notions of emotional "authenticity," affective and sense memory as "retrievals of past truths," and objectified notions of the self; when the actor is freed from the idea that there is a singular, "objective" authentic self, past or otherwise, to engage, she can more freely explore the possibilities of the self-in-the-now of the rehearsal or performance. The teacher's or coach's goal becomes to aid the actor not in being more "honest" or "connected to her truth," but in being more adept at what Michael calls "psycho-affective improvisations related to the scene or play."

In one of our conversations Michael noted that there isn't much detail or example in American translations of Stanislavsky's writing about how imagination might be used by the actor in a moment-by-moment, word-by-word way. He was particularly struck by the way the use of image streams could fill a lacuna in Stanislavsky's methods, by providing a technique for translating Stanislavsky's principles related to imagination on a "micro" level; it becomes a neurocognitively grounded application of the idea of the *kinolenta*. The use of image streams also counteracts those elements in US actor training that emphasize the actor's personal "material" while overlooking the importance of imagination. Michael works with this in his senior BFA acting class, focusing on Shakespeare, and in his directing. He has students in the class perform sonnets as a kind of character monologue; prior to encountering this research, Michael required students to develop a complete "discursive" paraphrase or narrative for the sonnet before having them move on to more "poetic" aspects of the piece. Now he moves quickly and relatively directly to question the actor word-by-word to be sure she or he has a connection to each moment and image in the sonnet; the idea is that the narrative will fill itself in as the images become articulated. What he has observed is an immediate payoff in terms of the actor's personalization of the material; this is precisely what is described by Ellen Locy in her work on *Boy Gets Girl*—the images begin to provide the narrative after a certain point, rather than vice versa. In directing Timberlake Wertenbaker's *Our Country's Good*, Michael spent time guiding actors to "see" or experience specific images related to their work, by setting up what he describes as "an imaginative technical rehearsal in their heads." He would require the actors to locate themselves as completely as possible in the world of the play and its givens in images, and to create givens and images where there were gaps in the script so that every moment was consciously filled in. This is not just about reason or analysis (though this is surely one of the things out of which vivid imagining grows), but about the actor locating herself in a vividly and fully imagined world that is integrated with the worlds of her fellow actors.

Michael has been involved in recruiting for BFA and MFA acting programs for many years. What he has learned about cognitive neuroscience and its possible implications for acting, through our conversations and his work in the studio and classroom, has led him to redefine what he thinks of as "talent"—the thing that catches him when watching the audition of a young person and makes him say, "Ah, *there's* an actor." Michael proposes that we set up new parameters for assessing an actor's potential and diagnosing where the actor needs to be stretched and challenged. He posits that talent might more accurately—and simply—be defined as "the ability to embody what is imagined," and I would not disagree. The issue becomes not how vulnerable, passionate, emotive, or smart actors are, but how easily and fully they enter into a theatrical world, and how freely their imaginations allow them to embody it. If the imagination is there—supported by solid technical training and will—, it will be more likely that all the rest will follow.

Afterword

I have two hopes for this book: that it has practical use in the studio and in performance for actors and that it makes a contribution to performance theory. Developments occur almost daily that have profound effects on how we understand ourselves, and that are already moving beyond the ideas in this book. In particular, ongoing research into neural systems related to mirroring and simulation (including, but not limited to, research on mirror neurons) is raising major questions about the nature of imitation, simulation, empathy, intention, the roots of language, and the connections not just within, but among our brains. What really is the nature of the boundaries between ourselves and others, between experience and imagination, between action and emotion, when observing the actions of another person lights up a set of neurons in our head identical to the one doing the acting?

Research on the neural level, though currently limited in terms of immediate practical applications for the actor, opens up fascinating and important questions. Vittorio Gallese, Giacomo Rizzolatti, and others assert select neural mechanisms "allow us to directly understand the meaning of the actions and emotions of others [we are observing] by internally replicating ('simulating') them without any explicit reflective mediation," i.e., without any conscious thought (Gallese, Keysers, Rizzolatti 2004: 396). These simulation mechanisms allow us to "link 'I do and I feel' with 'he does and he feels,'" and provide the basis for us to be able to function socially, i.e., in relationship to others. Through neural mirroring, even though we are not physically active, "part of our mirror system becomes active 'as if' we were executing that very same action that we are observing" (Gallese, Keysers, Rizzolatti 2004: 397). The resonances with Stanislavsky's "if" are obvious. Among other things, certain kinds of neural mirroring also allow us to understand the intentions of the person we are observing, i.e., we experience not just what they are doing, but to some degree what they want, "the 'why' of an action"—what actors might call motive (Iacoboni, Molnar-Szakacs *et al.* 2005: 0529). There is disagreement about how involved the motor mirror neuron system is in social cognition, which includes the perceptions of the intention or feeling behind a physical act (see particularly Jacob and Jeannerod 2006 and Csibra 2006), i.e., some scientists refuse to nickname mirror neurons "empathy neurons" or "Dalai Lama neurons," as some have. While Rizzolatti *et al.* argue that a mirroring mechanism "is also involved in our capacity to *understand* and *experience* the emotional states of others," as demonstrated in their research on the neural effects of observing facial expressions of disgust (Gallese, Keysers, Rizzolatti 2004: 397), Alvin Goldman hypothesizes that there are in fact three mechanisms that support mirroring and simulation: motoring mirroring mechanisms, general mirroring mechanisms, and simulational mechanisms, which work partly at the conscious level (Goldman 2006); this system provides linkages among pre- and conscious levels, which makes it, Goldman argues, "more promising as a unifying basis of social cognition." Regardless, we do know that much of this—whether categorized as mirroring or simulation—happens automatically, i.e., preconsciously.

While this work is related to Ekman's and Bloch's research on larger-scale physical phenomena and to Damasio's on "as-if" body states and emotion, it goes at least one crucial step further. In defining brain structures "that are active both during [sic] the first- and third-person experience of actions and emotions," i.e., the "I do/feel" and "he does/feels," a fundamental *physical* "bridge is created between others and ourselves" (Gallese, Keysers, Rizzolatti 2004: 400). What it posits is an "unmediated resonance" between individuals:

> The other's emotion is constituted, experienced and therefore directly understood by means of an embodied simulation producing a shared direct experiential understanding.
>
> By means of a shared neural state realized in two different bodies that nevertheless obey to the same morpho-functional rules, the "objectual other" becomes "another self."
>
> (Gallese 2006)

These are essentially definitions of empathy, and they begin to allow us to understand the mechanisms and different levels by which we identify with and connect to "others." Indeed, research has shown that the absence or defective functioning of mirroring systems is characteristic of autistic individuals, who are unable to connect socially or empathetically with others. Scientists are also considering prediction and "mind-reading" (in terms of reading the state or intention of another person) in regard to mirroring and simulation systems. Gergely Csibra hypothesizes that mirror neurons are "involved in the prediction or anticipation of subsequent—rather than in the simulation of concurrent—actions of the observed individual" (Csibra 2006), possibly making them more accurately named "predictor" neurons. This opens up new ways of thinking about a range of issues related to acting, including the functions and uses of basic mirror exercises in acting class, not to mention Meisner's repetition exercise. It also begins to provide a new way of conceptualizing the problem of anticipation in the actor's performance, allowing us to create new ways to address it with the knowledge that we are in fact "wired" to anticipate; the science may direct us toward new ways of getting around this.

We have accepted as a truism for some time that there is no hard and fast line between the conscious and preconscious. What is clear is that there is much more to the preconscious than the master acting teachers of the twentieth century might have imagined. Our growing understanding of the deep levels at which mirroring and simulation function is beginning to erase the habitual and comfortable lines we have constructed between self and other and between imagination (in terms of a neural pattern being the physical manifestation of an image) and action—for action and perception are in some aspects identical in the minds of the actor and the observer.

Some of the more radical extrapolations of the implications of this work are found in "Mirror Neurons and the Brain in the Vat," in which V. S. Ramachandran hypothesizes that the evolutionary development of mirror neurons about 100 to 200 thousand years ago allowed the human brain to become "*specialized* for culture" and "the organ of cultural diversity par excellence," because they allowed the rapid spread of cultural memes through mirroring and imitation. He concludes by stating that "the very notion of a *separate* 'you' or 'I' is an illusion, like the passage of time itself. We are all merely many reflections in a hall of mirrors of a single cosmic reality" (Ramachandran 2006). This statement leaves science behind for the theological or metaphysical, but I believe we must consider it at least to some degree. If we and our brains are connected—or even inseparable—in this way, what does it mean for those of us in the theatre to be part of an art that was founded on communion? What does it mean for that part of theatre that also has conflict, or even violence, within or between characters as a core attribute?

We must be open to the uses of science in regard to art in this time, when science and its rigorous application are being pervasively resisted politically and culturally by some of those in power in the US. If the purpose of theatre is, as Shakespeare wrote, to "hold a mirror up to nature," then we are duty bound to see and embrace those things that constitute nature as fully and honestly as possible. Part of this nature is that we are biological creatures with consciousnesses; we are constrained by organic processes that unfold in particular ways, and we are guided by cultural processes that interact contingently to direct the biological. As we learn more about this and, indeed, as the science increasingly lets us shape and control the biological, we may have to give up parts of old definitions of what a character or a feeling or a memory is, but this should only free us to be more flexible, powerful, and sensitive in the way that we make theatre.

The ultimate test of the thinking here is in its application in the studio or on stage—how do things fadge when you, the actor, are confronted with the reality of a thorny or seemingly opaque moment, or with resistance from a scene partner? How does this research help unlock the body and, thereby, the imagination—in the actor and in the audience? As Bertolt Brecht, that great admirer of Stanislavsky, said, "The proof of the pudding is in the eating."

Translation

Image, action, and Chekhov's
The Seagull

A particular set of problems of engaging image and action is involved in working with scripts in translation. Most of the texts discussed in Chapter 4 are originally in English, so there is no layer of linguistic translation between actor and script (apart from the personal and cultural "translating" we are doing any time we read a play). But since, in theatre, speech is embodied, we must take into account the specificity of word, sound, imagery, cultural and private associations, syntax, and rhythm that all work together to guide an actor in a particularly detailed way. It is possible to test the interconnected processes of language, mind, image, and action by examining the potential impact of different translations of a play on the actor, for even minor differences in translation can have a major effect on how an actor receives and understands a given character both in general, impressionistic terms and in moment-by-moment ones. While this is most obviously about cognition, it is equally as much about the neural nets that hold our memories and personal histories and experiences, and the way that language works on and through the body. What follows is a consideration of issues of translation as they relate to the actor's ability to imagine, activate, and embody character, action, and tone, and how these play out in a number of translations of one of Nina's speeches from Act IV of Chekhov's *The Seagull*.

There is no such thing as "the" definitive translation of a play, though there may be translations that serve a specific time and place particularly well, e.g., it is commonly held that Richard Wilbur's translations of Molière are definitive for our time in their skillfulness and beauty in transforming the originals' language, humanity, wit, energy, and rhythm into contemporary English. However, Wilbur's translations, as fine as they are, are not Molière. A one-to-one correlation between original and translation, or "equivalency," as it is called in translation studies, has long been shown to be an impossibility, and in the 1980s was roundly dismissed by translation scholars such as Susan Bassnett. Literal translation, in which there is an "authentic" or absolutely correct transposition from one language/culture into another, is unattainable because of the complex play of grammatical structures, vocabulary, and historico-cultural and personal associations with words, phrases, and syntax. Even a translation that follows the gross narrative of a text "faithfully" can drastically alter the deeper narrative of the piece, i.e., the dimension of it that has as much to do with what it might mean and feel like as with "what happens." It is entirely possible for one "literal" translation of a script to use descriptive language and have a detached tone, while another can use language that the characters actively direct toward each other; it is often a minor, but consequential, shift in perspective or emphasis. Part of what the actor reads a translation for is its content—the basic outline of what happens. But equally as important is reading for what Antonio Damasio might call "the *feeling* of what happens," as conveyed by the translation.

Translators who come from a background in literature or literary studies can have little experience of the practicalities of theatrical production or embodying a play in performance. These trans-lators sometimes take an approach that stops with the conception of a text as something literary, to be read rather than performed with an intense specificity that is physical and affective, as well as intellectual. Translations can miss some of the theatrical and per-formative dimensions of a text; while having merit and usefulness, these translations often present problems for the actor because they miss the character's "body." Conversely, though playwrights who claim to "translate" a script without knowing the original language may be familiar with theatre practice, they can take liberties with the text that remove it from key elements in the original. I believe it is more accurate to describe these texts as "adaptations" or "versions," especially when they are written by established playwrights with well known voices or characteristics of their own; they become a melding of the visions of the original and the adapter, e.g., Chekhov's *Uncle Vanya* becomes something some-what different when it becomes Mamet's. Bassnett recounts an instance of Michael Frayn, a well known and very good playwright who sometimes adapts others' scripts, asserting that there is no need to go to the original in order to understand the original:

> . . . in a debate on theatre translation at the Lyttleton Theatre in October 1989, [Frayn] declared that Chekhov is universal: "The good thing about Chekhov is that you don't need to know a word of Russian to be able to translate his plays because everyone knows what Chekhov is about, everyone knows by some sort of inner certainty what Chekhov intended and what he was saying, and the idea of referring it to some original text is absolutely odious." Frayn has, with astonishing arrogance, assumed that the English language can access the Russian regardless of linguistic or cultural difference. "Everyone," he claims, understands Chekhov, and understands not only the plays as written, but also the author's intentions.
>
> (Bassnett 1998: 93)

(There is the even more extreme example of playwrights who adapt others' texts for their own purposes, e.g., *The Notebook of Trigorin*, Tennessee Williams's "free adaptation" of *The Seagull*, in which, among other things, Trigorin is bisexual and fools around with Yakov the workman.)

The welter of images one deals with in addressing translation operates on a number of levels. There is the initial task of translating for narrative or literal "accuracy," in order to be sure the fundamental elements of the text are addressed. Depending upon the script, there can be synchronic and diachronic concerns in this initial pass, i.e., translating across space (from country to country or culture to culture) and across time (from a past era to today). In translating Chekhov, one is dealing with linguistic, cultural, and chronological differences. The grammatical and syntactic differences between languages deeply affect the possible ways in which an actor can visualize and enter into a play. For example, Russian verbs of motion, with their many roots and prefixes, allow greater specificity than English (there are different words for whether you are going on foot or by vehicle, and whether you will be returning), yet, on the other hand, Russians rarely use the present tense form of "to be." Another difference between Russian and English that has profound implications for the actor's imagination is the lack in Russian of articles (i.e., "a," "an," "the"). Consider what this means just for the titles of Chekhov's plays: is it *The Seagull* or *A Seagull*?

The Three Sisters or *Three Sisters*? *The Cherry Orchard* or *A Cherry Orchard*? The shifts among definite, indefinite, and no articles change the emphasis and the relationship one's imagination has to the play's material. One could assume, given the structure of the plays, that Chekhov intended that the definite article be understood. And what of the moments in Act IV of *The Seagull* in which Nina calls herself "seagull." What she literally says in these instances is "I seagull," leaving a number of choices to be made, e.g., "I am a seagull" as opposed to "I'm the seagull," that create strikingly different associations. (The Russian *chaika* refers to "gull" in general, not necessarily seagulls only. I choose to keep the translation of the word as "seagull" for three reasons. It is the standard translation of the word in relationship to this script; the word "gull" has associations in English that are counter to the idea of the bird to which the word refers; and "seagull" retains the two-syllable sound of the original.)

The sensory, sensual, and physical differences in sounds between languages also lead the actor to different feeling associations with words, phrases, speeches, and character. These are characteristics related to sound formation, rhythm, pitch, and general "texture." In short, different languages feel different not only in actors' bodies as they speak them, e.g., it feels different to say "I am the seagull" than "Ia chaika," but also in the mind. This psychophysical aspect of speech is as important as the intellectual or affective (this was touched on in the discussion of *Hamlet* in Chapter 4). This goes beyond the sense of aurality associated with onomatopoeia. When you act, you feel the language in your mouth, head, and torso—different words and sounds resonate in different ways physically as well as emotionally. Think about all the different ways one might play a middle "C" on a piano, and then multiply that difference by the number of different ways different words for a same or similar thing might be said, e.g., "excited," "thrilled," "ecstatic," "aquiver," etc., and all the different associations for these words that all generally mean "excited," how these meanings and associations are altered by each change in context, and all the different ways that an actor might say these words.

Script translation is an act of not just communicating, but also constructing meanings. As with actors, at the foundations of playwrights' creativity are their own personal "image banks"—sets of perceptions and potentials for perception growing out of their particular make-up and particular experiences. Chekhov, as an educated Russian at the turn of the last century, had associations with "chaika" different from those of a modern Russian, both of which are different from a modern American's associations with "seagull." In this regard the challenge of a good translation is to set up a structure that allows a kind of communion—not just "communication"—between the hypothetical mind of the original author and the mind of the actor. The good translation strings together a set of meanings, rhythms, and sounds that approximate, as well as possible, the main literal and associative meanings of the original text and which have a spoken, physical nature that engages the actor with that text. Ultimately, translation is always adaptation/adjustment/transformation; in the same way that a mental image is not the thing being imaged, the thing translated is never the thing itself. The best a translation can be is an effective and evocative "specific approximation."

In translation studies this raises the issue of "performability." Bassnett offers the following critique:

> English has tended to confound the act of translating a playtext across languages with the act of transposing a written text onto the stage. Discussion of the problems of translating theatre texts has tended to confuse these two quite separate processes. [. . .] It may, of course, be true that one translation works better than another, but there will always be many factors involved which can range from simple incompetence on the part of a translator to changes in the expectations of the target readership and divergence in theatre or social systems. [. . .] It is also significant that the term "performability" appears to emerge at the same time as the naturalist drama, and is consequently linked to ideas of consistency in characterisation and to the notion of the gestural subtext.
>
> (Bassnett 1998: 95)

There are two aspects of translation/transposition here: the literary/linguistic and the theatrical, which Bassnett defines as being involved whenever someone performs a written text. Her linking of "performability" to "ideas of [psychological] consistency in characterisation and to the notion of the gestural subtext" is understandable, given some actors' attachment to a narrow, even comfortable (because habitual) sense of psychological realism and overly formulaic or essentialist sense of character or subtext. For these actors, subtexts might more accurately be called "self-texts," for they come out of a personal comfort zone of familiarity that says more about the limitations of the actor's imagination than a set of actual and potential meanings in the script. (Such issues of authorship and authority are not limited to translated texts; even when dealing with English-language scripts, some actors consciously or unconsciously rewrite elements in a script to make it fit more closely to their habits of performance.)

There are numerous readings or "subtexts" to any good script, not a single gestural or Ur-subtext, because the words on the page are only a trace between the bodies and consciousnesses of the author and the actor, a means of transmitting an experience from one individual who writes to another who makes a multitude of choices about how to make that trace as palpable as possible through her own body. Working in translation further complicates the choice-making process, multiplying the possible choices through two languages and two cultures, often across time and history. Because this is so, it is more fruitful to view "performability" in translations as being detached from ideas of realism or gestural subtext and connected to a rigorous attention to specificity and nuance in meaning (or "content") and to formal, physical expressiveness—the specific words, sounds, and rhythms used to convey those meanings. This is related to much of what is discussed in Chapter 4, with the addition of cross-cultural and cross-linguistic components.

Chekhov is one of the most beloved, most challenging, and most misunderstood playwrights in the canon. The complexity of his tone—marrying elements of comedy, tragedy, farce, and melodrama—and the intricacy of his structures are unlike those of any other author. Each line in his plays forms a part of a complex web of relationships—of character, action, and theme. Too often English-language translations and performances miss the full richness of the plays, sometimes by stressing a comic or serious "wash" or failing to connect the dots—to see the network—of the script. The detail, complexity, and emotional fullness of Chekhov's writing make it an ideal case in the argument for a neurocognitive approach to performance. Devising a full and complete image stream, uniting each moment and reference in the play, can be especially fruitful in approaching this material.

Chekhov presents some particular problems for the translator. We find ourselves in a situation similar to the Russians with Shakespeare—we have the benefit and the challenge of being able to do a diachronic (across time) as well as synchronic (across space) translation, transforming the syntax and vocabulary of the plays to accommodate the changing times as well as the different languages. Laurence Senelick's "Chekhov's Plays in English" succinctly covers basic issues related to Chekhov's language and the challenges of translating it into English. Among the major points he cites are:

1   Chekhov's use of recurrent phrases for irony and resonance, of literary allusions, of subliminal lexical and etymological elements;
2   The particular cadence with which each character speaks;
3   The particular ways in which sentences are structured to reveal character, which go beyond mere literal translation;
4   The historically specific associations of certain words and phrases;
5   The difficulty of translating specifically Russian structures such as "passive constructions [. . .], verbs of imperfect action and onomatopoeic sounds that are overlooked or scanted."

(Senelick 2000: 11)

To this last I would also add the absence of articles in Russian, as mentioned earlier, the presence of formal and familiar pronominal forms (similar to "vous" and "tu" in French, "usted" and "tu" in Spanish, and "Sie" and "du" in German), and a more nuanced form of personal address (involving the use of first names, patronymics, surnames, and diminutives).

A comparison of translations of a segment of Nina's Act IV speech in *The Seagull* reveals the range of different feelings and associations possible even among translations that can mean relatively the same thing literally or factually. Translation choices affect the sense of how a piece might be interpreted and embodied by an actor, i.e., how a translation can determine to a large degree the images that are activated in an actor's being. Aspects to consider in evaluating how the various translations guide the actor include literal meaning (the gross "what happens" of the play); character intention (subtler aspects of action that often have to do with subtext and which therefore often say more about the actor and less about the "truth" or intention in a text); explicit and implicit imagery and associations; intensity (related to intention and having to do with how the text leads the actor–reader to understand the focus and passion of a character's speech); and qualitative and structural aspects related to musicality, i.e., the physical feeling of the speech in the body (rhythm, tone, texture, duration). I've picked this particular segment of text because it includes some of the most well known and challenging lines in the play, and many a young woman has foundered trying to make them theatrically effective and moving.

What follows is the Russian, very roughly transliterated, but I hope it provides a sense of the sounds and rhythms of the text, and as literal a translation as possible:

Ya—chaika. Nyet, ne to . . . Pomnitye, vy podstrelili chaiku? Sluchaino prishol chelovek, uvidel i ot nichevo delat' pogubil . . . syuzhet dlya nebolshovo rasskaza. Eto ne to . . . (Tret sebye lob.) O chyom ya? . . . Ya govoryu o stsene. Teper' uzh ya ne tak . . . Ya uzhe nastoyashchaya aktrisa, ya igrayo s naslazhdeniem, s vostorgom, p'yaneyu na stsene i chuvstvuyu sebya prekrasnoi. A teper', poka zhivy zdes', ya vse khozhy peshkom, vse khozhy i dumayu, dumayu i chuvstvuyu, kak s kazhdym dhyom rastut moi dushevniye sily . . . Ya teper' znayu, ponimayu, Kostya, chto v nashem dele—vsyo ravno, igraem mi na tsene ili pishem—glavnoe ne slava, ne blesk, ne to, o chom ya mechtala, a umen'e terpet'. Umei nesti svoi krest' i veruy. Ya veruyu, i mne ne tak bol'no, i kogda ya dumayu o svoyom prizvanii, to ne boyus' zhizni.

I [am]—[the/a] seagull. No, not that . . . Remember, you shot [a/the] seagull? There happened to come along [a] man, [he] saw it and from nothing to do killed it . . . a subject for [a] not-big story. That [is] not it . . . (Rubs herself on [the] forehead.) About what [am/was] I? . . . I [am] talking about [the] stage. Now already I [am] not so . . . I [am] already [a] real/genuine actress, I act with joy/delight, with ecstasy, I [am] drunk on [the] stage and feel myself beautiful. And now, while [I] live/am here, I always walk on foot, walk and think, think and feel, as though with every day grows my spiritual strength . . . I now know, [you] understand, Kostya, that in our business—it [is] all the same, we act on [the] stage or [we] write—[the] main thing is not glory, not fame, not that, about which I dreamed, but to endure. To carry your cross and believe. I believe, and for me it [is] not so bad, and when I think of/about my calling, then I [am] not afraid of life.

(Chekhov n.d.: 191–192)

The following five approaches to this text, apart from Constance Garnett's, whose was the standard for many prior to the 1960s, are those of selected major playwrights or theatrical translators. Parenthetical phrases following each translator indicate how the text was defined and the year in which it was published.

Constance Garnett (translated by; 1923)

I am a sea-gull. No, that's not it. . . . Do you remember you shot a sea-gull? A man came by chance, saw it and, just to pass the time, destroyed it. . . . A subject for a short story. . . . That's not it, though *(rubs her forehead)*. What was I saying? . . . I am talking of the stage. Now I am not like that. I am a real actress, I act with enjoyment, with enthusiasm, I am intoxicated when I am on the stage and feel that I am splendid. And since I have been here, I keep walking about and thinking, thinking and feeling that my soul is getting stronger every day. Now I know, I understand, Kostya, that in our work—in acting or writing—what matters is not fame, not glory, not what I dreamed of, but knowing how to be patient. To bear one's cross and have faith. I have faith and it all doesn't hurt so much, and when I think of my vocation I am not afraid of life.

(Chekhov, trans. Garnett 1923: 56–57)

Unsurprisingly, in the Garnett translation there is a datedness, an awkwardness of voice to modern ears, e.g., as evidenced in the absence of contractions. The syntax of "feel that I am splendid" is formal and proper. Safe, or denatured, choices continue with the substitution of "enthusiasm" for the more erotic "ecstasy" or "rapture" typically used for *vostorg*. "Vocation" is technically correct for the Russian *prizvanie*, but "calling" is also accurate and has richer connotations and liquid sounds that more effectively convey the openness and transcendence that I believe are important aspects of this moment. On the whole, Garnett's tone tends toward the descriptive and literary, which would in likelihood lead the actress playing Nina to a proper, rather contained interpretation, lacking the emotional complexity and power of the original. As happens in many translations, the choice of the indefinite article in the phrase "a seagull" detaches the image from the event in the play to which it hearkens back: Treplev's shooting of the seagull and laying at Nina's feet, followed by Trigorin's making note of the beautiful, dead bird as an image for a story about a beautiful, betrayed girl. This generalized reference inhibits the actor playing Nina from making as strong a psychophysical connection as possible between the moments in Act II and the moments in Act IV.

Jean Claude Van Itallie (English version; 1994)

> I'm a sea gull. No, that's not what I mean . . . Do you remember once you shot a sea gull? A man came along, saw a sea gull, and destroyed it for fun . . . That's a subject for a short story . . . No, that's not what I mean . . . *(She touches her forehead, rubs it.)* What was I saying? My acting. I'm not like that now. I'm a real actress. I enjoy it, I revel in it. I'm intoxicated on stage, and feel beautiful there. Ever since I've been home I've been walking, walking and thinking, feeling my mind and spirit getting stronger every day . . . I know now, Kostya, what matters in our work. What matters for a writer or an actor is not fame, glory, or the things I dreamed about, but knowing how to endure—how to bear your cross and have faith. I have faith now, and it's not so painful anymore. When I think about my calling, I'm not afraid of life.
>
> (Chekhov, trans. Van Itallie 1994: 48–49)

Van Itallie's "a seagull" misses the mark in the same way that Garnett's does. "No, that's not what I mean" changes both the rhythm and meaning of the Russian, especially in terms of Nina's (and thereby the actor's) thought processes. In the first instance the Russian is *Eto ne to*, "That's not it," which is simpler and more percussive (note the sounds). In the second instance the Russian is *Nyet, ne to*, "No, not that," which is even more emphatic in its repetition and rejection of the thought. I could also argue that Van Itallie's syntax here directs the actor outward, possibly toward

Kostya, at a moment in which the Russian indicates Nina is more focused on correcting and clarifying her thoughts for herself. The interpretation of Nina implied by this translation seems to make her more egocentric than is indicated in the original. Here she says, "[I was talking about] My acting," instead of "I'm talking about the stage"; while the latter implies something larger, connected to Nina's sense of calling, the former is focused more on herself. The path for the actor's imagination would be charted very differently by these two choices. In a similar vein, Van Itallie's use of "been home" is, in terms of its associations, a departure from the original, in which Nina refers only to being back. This considerably alters the actor's sense of how Nina understands her return to the lake: the emotional charge or resonance of saying "home" in any context can be very loaded; in this context—in which Nina has been abandoned by her father and in which she has no place to call home—it is particularly loaded and, I believe, misleading. Van Itallie alters the flow of the last lines of the speech by inserting full stops, or periods, where there are only commas in the Russian; this shift in rhythm changes the sense of the depth of Nina's conviction and the strength of urgency in her desire to persuade Kostya that she is alright. These additional stops indicate more discrete units of thought, a calculation or an effort, rather than a sense that she is speaking openly and flowingly from the heart, as seems to be indicated by the original. However, Van Itallie's translation has a better sense of clarity, flow, and accuracy than Garnett's from an actor's point of view.

Tom Stoppard (a new version; 1997)

The seagull. No, that's *not* me . . . You remember how you once shot that seagull? A man happened to come along and see her, and having nothing much to do, destroyed her. Idea for a short story . . . Wrong story, though. What was I talking about? Yes, about acting. I'm not like that any more. I've become a real actress. I love acting, when I'm on stage I feel drunk on the sheer joy of it, and I feel beautiful. While I've been back here I've spent a lot of time walking and thinking—and every day I've felt my spirit getting stronger. What I've realized, Kostya, is that, with us, whether we're writers or actors, what really counts is not dreaming about fame and glory . . . but stamina:

knowing how to keep going despite everything, and having faith
in yourself—I've got faith in myself now and that's helped the
pain, and when I think to myself, "You're on the stage!", then
I'm not afraid of anything life can do to me.

(Chekhov, trans. Stoppard 1997: 68–69)

Stoppard's use of the definite article for "the seagull" allows the actor
to make a much more specific connection with the image, grounded
in prior given circumstances of the play. (Though he is a native of
the former Czechoslovakia, Stoppard left his homeland at such a
young age that he didn't learn Russian, as would have been typical
for Eastern bloc children at the time.) However, he takes considerable liberties with Nina's self-corrections, turning "That's not
it" into "Wrong story, though," just as, in the lines immediately
preceding those quoted, he turns "Not that" and "No, not that"
into "but I'm not really" and "No, that's *not* me." Stoppard eliminates the repetitive thought/word pattern of these phrases, which are
part of the music of the scene, and substitutes some cleverness and
variety for Chekhov's simple evocation of Nina's struggle to gain
some clarity. The hesitation in Chekhov's syntax, "About what was
I? . . . I'm talking about the stage" is cleaned up with "What was I
talking about? Yes, about acting"; this shifts the sense of emphasis
and where the mental clarity is in these phrases. There is another
subtle, but meaningful, shift when Stoppard changes "[the] main
thing is not glory, not fame, not that about which I dreamed" to
"what really counts is not dreaming about fame and glory"; the
focus in the Russian is explicitly on fame and glory, and secondarily
on dreams, but the translation softens the strength of the original.
This translation also eliminates the sense of spirituality and faith in
the latter part of the speech. It uses the problematic "stamina" for
"patience"; inserts the phrase "in yourself" after "having faith,"
which in the Russian implicitly refers to faith in something grander;
and eliminates the reference to carrying one's cross. The Russian
sense of "faith" or "belief" here has associations with a larger
cultural sense of connectedness and soulfulness. The egocentricity,
even narcissism, of this Nina is reinforced by the substitution of
"when I think to myself, 'You're on the stage!'" for "when I think
of my calling." Counter to what is explicit at least in the rhetoric
in the Russian original, Stoppard's Nina has not outgrown her naive
dreams of fame, and she has not arrived at a more mature sense

of life and the artists' calling. He goes beyond Van Itallie in overdetermining Nina as narcissistic and materialistic. The actress given this translation would be led to a sense of Nina in Act IV as a worldly, self-centered survivor.

Paul Schmidt (a new translation; 1997)

> I'm the seagull. . . . No, that's not it. . . . Remember that seagull you shot? A man comes along, sees her, and destroys her life because he has nothing better to do . . . subject for a short story. No, that's not it. . . . *(Rubs her forehead)* What was I saying? Oh, yes, the theater . . . I'm not like that anymore. I'm a real actress now, I enjoy acting, I'm proud of it, the stage intoxicates me. When I'm up there I feel beautiful. And these days, being back here, walking for hours on end, thinking and thinking, I could feel my soul growing stronger day after day. And now I know, Kostya, I understand, finally, that in our business—acting, writing, it makes no difference—the main thing isn't being famous, it's not the sound of applause, it's not what I dreamed it was. All it is is the strength to keep going, no matter what happens. You have to keep on believing. I believe, and it helps. And now when I think about my vocation, I'm not afraid of life.
>
> (Chekhov, trans. Schmidt 1997: 158–159)

Schmidt uses the more specific "the seagull," but his "Remember that seagull you shot?" for "Remember, you shot [a/the] seagull?" is a small, but possibly important shift from remembering an object to remembering an action; i.e., remembering killing an animal is different from remembering the animal killed. Rather than using the accurate "glory," real liberties are taken in using "the sound of applause," which is nowhere in Chekhov and which diminishes the nature of Nina's old dreams. Schmidt has a new twist with "the strength to keep going, no matter what happens. You have to keep on believing," instead of "to endure. To bear your cross and have faith." Schmidt rightly captures a sense of endurance, but the larger spiritual sense of the effort is less than in the Russian. Nonetheless, Schmidt's Nina is both in pain and relatively lucid, struggling to make a good go of her life—an appropriate, complex, grounded choice.

The following is my attempt to be as faithful as possible to the Russian, making choices with an eye toward translating the beauty of this passage for a contemporary American actor. A myriad of other choices are possible with this material, so I offer this version as food for thought, not just in translating Chekhov, but in thinking about how even the smallest variations in text and language matter in guiding the actor in constructing a private score, a personal stream of images, for a role:

> I'm—the seagull. No, that's not it . . . Remember, you shot a seagull? A man happened to come along, he saw it, and out of nothing better to do, he destroyed it . . . A subject for a short story. That's not it . . . *Rubs her forehead.* What was I—? . . . I'm talking about the stage. Now I'm not like that . . . Now I'm a real actress, I act with joy, with ecstasy, I'm intoxicated when I'm on stage and I feel beautiful. And now, since I've been here, I've been walking everywhere, walking and thinking, thinking and feeling the strength in my soul growing every day . . . Now I know, I understand, Kostya, that in our work it's all the same whether you act or write—the main thing is not fame, not glory, not what I dreamed of, but to endure. To bear one's cross and have faith. I have faith and it's not so bad any more, and when I think of my calling, I'm not afraid of life.

The translation attempts to be as direct and simple as Chekhov—true to literal meanings and punctuation in the Russian, and as true as possible to the affective and tonal world of the text, in order to convey the sense of the original as much as possible—and to serve the actor's embodiment.

The first sentence—"I'm—the seagull"—chooses the definite article and preserves the break in thought indicated by the dash in the original. The meaning of this hesitation is open to many interpretations: it could imply resistance, fear, a struggle to find the right word. But fundamentally it implies *something* happening in the moment before Nina says "seagull." In the Russian, some kind of psychic event occurs before Nina completes her thought. On a performative level, in terms of the feeling and image, "I'm—the seagull" differs measurably from " I am a sea-gull," "I'm a sea gull," "The seagull," or "I'm the seagull."

Similarly, it would be very different for an actress to work with these five variations of the same phrase: "What was I saying? . . . I am talking of the stage." (12 syllables, 2 complete sentences, 2 full stops interrupted by an ellipsis); "What was I saying? My acting." (8 syllables, 1 sentence, 1 phrase, 2 full stops); "What was I talking about? Yes, about acting." (12 syllables, 1 sentence, 1 phrase, 2 full stops); "What was I saying? Oh, yes, the theater [sic]." (10 syllables, 1 sentence, 1 phrase, 2 full stops); "What was I—? I'm talking about the stage" (10 syllables, 1 truncated phrase, 1 sentence, 1 full stop). The last translation accounts for the truncation, and thereby the tenuousness, in the first part in Chekhov's original ("What was I —?"). Besides indicating an inner state of confusion, the broken phrase thwarts any fluid rhythm in its execution—an uncompleted thought and, hence, an uncompleted breath for the actor. There is, or should be, nothing new in this approach. A standard practice among actors who do Shakespeare is to study the various folios and quartos, which vary wildly. Differences in punctuation, spelling, capitalization can make significant differences in how a passage is understood, experienced, and performed by the actor, so there is never an assumption that what is published in a standard acting edition of Shakespeare is definitive. The second part of this phrase in the Russian ("I'm talking about the stage") is grounded and grammatically complete; it reclaims clarity. It refers specifically to the stage, not to acting or the theatre; it is about a concrete place, not about the act of performing or about an abstraction.

The translation I offer generally has punctuation closer to that in the Russian. It has fewer full stops, providing a sense of thought processes and internal energy which guide the actor in understanding the fluidity and contingency of Nina's inner life; there is no attempt to "neaten" up the punctuation, for what is in the original provides important information for the actor. The final sentence gives a sense of momentum, of rolling forward, which allows the actor to move through from "I have faith" to "I'm not afraid of life," grounded in a single breath or impulse, rather than being broken up, i.e., the thread is because she has faith, she is not afraid of life. The images and impulses cascade (to use Kagan's image from Chapter 1) over one another, tumbling out of Nina's heart and mind. These points are small, but they are basic, "brick-by-brick," moment-by-moment elements of the actor's work. An actor says a particular word—or she doesn't. She makes a particular gesture—or she doesn't. It is the accumulation of moments—the use of semi-stops in punctuations, rather than full stops, the use of the word "stage," rather than "theatre"—which in fact make up the performance.

Chekhov's specific, conversational syntax provides an actor with clear indications of a character's processes of thought and feeling, in terms of literal content, as well as less tangible, image- and rhythm-based impulses that are just as important to the "truth" of the character. Just as a piece of music is composed of specific notes and a dance of specific steps, the particular "notes" (e.g., syllables, sounds, punctuation, as well as literal meanings) in a translated phrase lead the actor to sing a different song, to continue the metaphor.

However, having invoked metaphors of music and dance, it is important to recognize the challenges in working with words (especially in translation), as opposed to notes or steps. Beginning with the basic challenge of working not only with a generalized or literal "what" (all reputable translations convey that Nina has had a hard life), the translator must address a more nuanced "what *and* how" that can determine the actor's understanding of the character's fundamental nature, i.e., what are the particulars of Nina's response to and experience of that hard life, and how is the actor constructing her personal images of that life? In fact, any translation's potential subtextual and paraverbal aspects direct the actor's sense of what is happening and how to interpret it. In a fundamental way, it affects one's sense of Nina as victim or survivor. Does the translator (or actor) begin with the premise that Nina has been struggling to maintain her sanity, even though the only reference in the text to support this view is Treplev's line in Act IV: "I began getting letters from [Nina] after I came home. Intelligent, warm, interesting letters. She didn't complain, but she seemed deeply unhappy. There wasn't a line that wasn't forced, troubled. And her imagination was a little crazy. She signed herself 'the Seagull' " (Blair, unpublished manuscript). Even here, it isn't Nina who is a little crazy, but her imagination. Or is the premise that, in this final scene, Nina is in understandable, very human *extremis*—not mad, but struggling with having a hard life and a challenging career path, having lost her baby, still loving Trigorin, and being tired, hungry, and thirsty *right now*—all things about which she speaks explicitly in the scene?

A few years ago I worked on a translation for a production of *The Cherry Orchard*. For a number of nights, the director, the entire cast (composed of MFA and BFA students), and I sat around a large table with Chekhov's original, a rough, literal translation, various Russian-English dictionaries, thesauruses, synonym dictionaries, and other English translations of the play. I provided expertise in Russian and various facts about Russian culture, and the actors and director brought in questions and observations gleaned from comparative readings of other English translations of the play. As we read through the play, moment-by-moment, various meanings of Russian words were discussed, issues of rhythm, syntax, and subtext were considered, and I gained a sense of each actor as a presence and as a potential player for his or her character. In this methodical, collaborative process, I believe all of us gained a richer sense of how to approach *The Cherry Orchard* in this particular case, and I know the actors were more connected personally to the text and images than they would have been otherwise. In some ways, this was not too different from Chekhov's writing of the original, for he wrote his last plays, at least in part, with particular actors in mind.

Developing a role in a play in translation is a quintessential instance of the way that performance is paradoxically both concrete and contingent. The material dimension of performance is determined by the particular words given to the actor and, among other things, the physical space of performance, the amount of time available to develop the performance, all of which constrain and guide the particular score—mental and physical—that each actor develops. The nature of that material experience changes dramatically depending upon the particular production, once one goes beyond the words and the general narrative. Given the specificities of bodies and of histories, translation is always adaptation/adjustment/transformation—the thing interpreted is never the thing itself.

Works consulted

Adler, S. (1988) *The Technique of Acting*, New York: Bantam Books.
—— (2000) *Stella Adler: The Art of Acting*, ed. H. Kissel, New York: Applause Books.
Alexander, F. M. (1984) *The Use of the Self: Its Conscious Direction in Relation to Diagnosis, Functioning and the Control of Reaction*, Long Beach, California: Centerline Press.
Artaud, A. (1958) *The Theater and Its Double*, trans. M. C. Richards, New York: Grove Press.
Baars, B. (1988) *A Cognitive Theory of Consciousness*, New York: Cambridge University Press.
—— (1997) *In the Theater of Consciousness: The Workspace of the Mind*, Oxford: Oxford University Press.
Bassnett, S. (1998) "Still Trapped in the Labyrinth: Further Reflections on Translation and Theatre," in S. Bassnett and A. Lefevere (eds) *Constructing Cultures: Essays on Literary Translation*, Clevedon, England: Multilingual Matters, 90–108.
Benedetti, J. (1988) *Stanislavski: A Biography*, New York: Routledge.
Benton, A. (2000) *Exploring the History of Neuropsychology: Selected Papers*, New York: Oxford University Press.
Blair, R. (2000) "The Method and the Computational Theory of Mind," in D. Krasner (ed.) *Method Acting Reconsidered: Theory, Practice, Future*. New York: St. Martin's Press, 201–218.
—— (2001) " 'Specific Approximations': Chekhov's *The Seagull*, Translation, and the Actor," *Metamorphosis: The Five Colleges Journal of Translation*, 148–164.
—— (2002) "Reconsidering Stanislavsky: Feeling, Feminism, and the Actor," *Theatre Topics* 12:2, 177–190.
—— (2006) "Image and Action: Cognitive neuroscience and actor training," in B. McConachie and F. E. Hart (eds) *Performance and Cognition: Theatre Studies and the Cognitive Turn*, New York: Routledge, 167–185.

Blakeslee, S. (2006) "Cells That Read Minds," *New York Times*, 10 January 2006. www.nytimes.com/2006/01/10/science/10mirr.html?ex=1138683600&en=b4ece2a93cbeb429&ei=5070.

Bloch, S. (1989) "Effector patterns of basic emotions: an experimental model for emotional induction," *Behavioral Brain Research* 33, 317.

—— (1993) "ALBA Emoting: A Psychophysiological Technique to Help Actors Create and Control Real Emotions," *Theatre Topics* 3:2, 121–138.

—— and Lemeignan, M. (1992) "Precise Respiratory-Posturo-Facial Patterns are Related to Specific Basic Emotions," *Bewegen und Hulpverlening* 1, 31–39.

——, Lemeignan, M., and Auguilera-Torres, N. (1991) "Specific Respiratory Patterns Distinguish Among Human Basic Emotions," *International Journal of Psychophysiology* 11, 141–154.

——, Orthous, P., and Santibañez-H, G. (1987) "Effector patterns of basic emotions: a psychophysiological method for training actors," *Journal of Social Biological Structure* 10, 1–19; reprinted in P. Zarrilli (ed.) (2nd edn 2002) *Acting (Re)Considered: A Theoretical and Critical Guide*, New York: Routledge.

—— and Santibañez-H, G. (1973) "Training emotional 'effection' in humans: significance of its feedback on subjectivity," in S. Bloch and R. Anieros (eds) *Psicobiologia del Aprendizaje*, Santiago: Publi. Fac. Med. Universite de Chile, 170–185.

Brecht, B. (1964) *Brecht on Theatre: The Development of an Aesthetic*, ed. J. Willett, New York: Hill and Wang.

Brennan, T. (2004) *The Transmission of Affect*, Ithaca: Cornell University Press.

Broca, P. (1861) "Perte de la parole," *Bulletins de la Société Anthropologique de Paris* 2, 235–238.

—— (1878) "Anatomie comparée des circonvolutions cérébrales," *Révue Anthropologique* 1, 385–498.

Butler, J. (1990) "Performative Acts and Gender Constitution: An Essay in Phenomenology and Feminist Theory," in S. Case (ed.) *Performing Feminisms*, Baltimore: The Johns Hopkins University Press, 270–282.

Carlson, M. (2nd edn 2004) *Performance: A Critical Introduction*, New York: Routledge.

Carnicke, S. M. (1993) "Stanislavsky: Uncensored and Unabridged," *TDR* 37.1, 22–37.

—— (1998) *Stanislavsky in Focus*, Amsterdam: Harwood Academic Publishers.

Chaikin, J. (1972) *The Presence of the Actor*, New York: Atheneum.

Chekhov, A. (n.d.) *P'ecy*, London: Bradda Books.

—— *The Seagull*, trans. Rhonda Blair, unpublished manuscript.

—— (1968) *Four Great Plays by Anton Chekhov*, trans. C. Garnett, New York: Bantam Books.

—— (1995) *Chekhov: The Major Plays*, trans. J. Van Itallie, New York: Applause Books.

—— (1997) *The Seagull*, trans. T. Stoppard, London: Faber & Faber.

—— (1998) *The Plays of Chekhov*, trans. P. Schmidt, New York: Harper Flamingo.

—— (2006) *Anton Chekhov: The Complete Plays*, trans. L. Senelick, New York: W. W. Norton.

Chekhov, M. (1953) *To the Actor: On the Technique of Acting*, New York: Harper.

Cole, T. (1947) *Acting: A Handbook of the Stanislavski Method*, New York: Crown Publishers.

Connolly, M. (2003–2006), personal conversations.

Conrad, H. (ed.) (2003) *The Development of Alba Emoting*, Idaho: Brigham Young University—Idaho.

Cook, A. (2006) "Staging Nothing: *Hamlet* and Cognitive Science," *SubStance* #110, Vol. 35, no. 2, 83–99.

Csibra, G. (2006) "Mirror neurons and action observation. Is simulation involved?" *Interdisciplines: What Do Mirror Neurons Mean?: Mirror Systems, Social Understanding and Social Cognition*, www.inter disciplines.org/mirror/papers/4.

Damasio, A. (1994) *Descartes' Error: Emotion, Reason and the Human Brain*, New York: Avon Books.

—— (1999) *The Feeling of What Happens: Body and Emotion in the Making of Consciousness*, New York: Harcourt Brace.

—— (2003) *Looking for Spinoza: Joy, Sorrow, and the Feeling Brain*, New York: Harcourt.

Davidson, R. J. (2001) "Toward a Biology of Personality and Emotion," in A. Damasio, A. Harrington, J. Kagan, B. S. McEwen, H. Moss, and R. Shaikh (eds) *Unity of Knowledge: The Convergence of Natural and Human Science*, New York: The New York Academy of Sciences, Vol. 935, 191–207.

Dennett, D. C. (1991) *Consciousness Explained*, Boston: Little, Brown.

—— (1995) *Darwin's Dangerous Idea: Evolution and the Meanings of Life*, New York: Simon & Schuster.

—— (2003) *Freedom Evolves*, New York: Viking.

Dickinson, E. (1960) *The Complete Poems of Emily Dickinson*, ed. T. H. Johnson, Boston: Little, Brown.

Diderot, D. (1994) "The Paradox of the Actor," *Dennis Diderot: Selected Writings on Art and Literature*, trans. and ed. G. Bremner, New York: Penguin Books.

Donald, M. (1991) *Origins of the Modern Mind: Three Stages in the Evolution of Culture and Cognition*, Cambridge, Massachusetts: Harvard University Press.

Edelman, G. M. (1987) *Neural Darwinism: The Theory of Neuronal Group Selection*, New York: Basic Books.

—— (1989) *The Remembered Present: A Biological Theory of Consciousness*, New York: Basic Books.

—— (2004) *Wider than the Sky: The Phenomenal Gift of Consciousness*, New Haven: Yale University Press.

—— (2006) *Second Nature: Brain Science and Human Knowledge*, New Haven: Yale University Press.

—— and Tononi, G. (2000) *A Universe of Consciousness: How Matter Becomes Imagination*, New York: Basic Books.

Ekman, P. (1992) "Facial expressions of emotions: New findings, new questions," *Psychological Science* 3, 34–38.

—— (2003) *Emotions Revealed: Recognizing Faces and Feelings to Improve Communication and Emotional Life*, New York: Times Books.

——, Campos, J., Davidson, R. J., and de Waal, F. B. M. (eds) (2003) *Emotions Inside Out: 130 Years after Darwin's* The Expression of Emotions in Man and Animals, New York: The New York Academy of Sciences.

Emigh, J. (2002) "Performance Studies, Neuroscience, and the Limits of Culture," in N. Stucky and C. Wimmer (eds) *Teaching Performance Studies*, Carbondale: Southern Illinois University Press, 261–276.

Fauconnier, G. and Turner, M. (2002) *The Way We Think: Conceptual Blending and the Mind's Hidden Complexities*, New York: Basic Books.

Feldenkreis, M. (1977) *Awareness Through Movement: Easy to do Health Exercises to Improve your Posture, Vision, and Imagination*, New York: Harper & Row.

Frijda, N. H., Manstead, A. S. R., and Bern, S. (eds) (2000) *Emotions and Beliefs: How Feelings Influence Thoughts*, Cambridge: Cambridge University Press.

Gallese, V. (2006) "Intentional Attunement. The Mirror Neuron system and its role in interpersonal relations," *Interdisciplines: What Do Mirror Neurons Mean?: Mirror Systems, Social Understanding and Social Cognition*, www.interdisciplines.org/mirror/papers/1.

——, Keysers, C, and Rizzolatti, G. (2004) "A unifying view of the basis of social cognition," *Trends in Cognitive Sciences*, Vol. 8, No. 9, Sept., 396–403.

Garfield, D. (1980) *A Player's Place: The Story of the Actors Studio*, New York: Macmillan.

Gazzaniga, M. S. (1988) *Mind Matters: How Mind and Brain Interact to Create Our Conscious Lives*, Boston: Houghton Mifflin.

—— (1992) *Nature's Mind: The Biological Roots of Thinking, Emotions, Sexuality, Language, and Intelligence*, New York: Basic Books.

—— (1998) *The Mind's Past*, Berkeley: University of California Press.

—— (2005) *The Ethical Brain*, New York: Dana Press.

Gilman, Rebecca (2002) *Boy Gets Girl*, New York: Faber & Faber.

Gilman, Richard (1995) *Chekhov's Plays: An Opening into Eternity*, New Haven: Yale University Press.

Gladkov, A. (1997) *Meyerhold Speaks, Meyerhold Rehearses*, trans. and ed. A. Law, Amsterdam: Harwood Academic Publishers.

Goldman, A. (2006) "Mirror Systems, Social Understanding and Social Cognition," *Interdisciplines: What Do Mirror Neurons Mean?: Mirror Systems, Social Understanding and Social Cognition*, www.inter disciplines.org/mirror/papers/3.

Gordon, R. M. (1987) *The Structure of Emotions: Investigations in Cognitive Philosophy*, Cambridge; New York: Cambridge University Press.

Gray, J. (2004) *Consciousness: Creeping Up on the Hard Problem*, New York: Oxford University Press.

Hagen, U. (1973) *Respect for Acting*, New York: Macmillan.

—— (1991) *A Challenge for the Actor*, New York: Scribner's.

Haraway, D. (1991) "A Cyborg Manifesto: Science, Technology, and Socialist-Feminism in the Late Twentieth Century," in *Simians, Cyborgs and Women: The Reinvention of Nature*, New York: Routledge, 149–181.

—— (1997) *Modest_Witness@Second_Millennium.FemaleMan©_Meets_ OncoMouse®: Feminism and Technoscience*, New York: Routledge.

Harrington, A., Deacon, T. W., Kosslyn, S. M., and Scarry, E. (2001) "Science, Culture, Meaning, Values: A Dialogue," in A. Damasio, A. Harrington, J. Kagan, B. S. McEwen, H. Moss, and R. Shaikh (eds), *Unity of Knowledge: The Convergence of Natural and Human Science*, New York: The New York Academy of Sciences, Vol. 935, 233–257.

Hodge, A. (2000) *Twentieth Century Actor Training*, New York: Routledge.

Hurley, S. L. (2006) "The shared circuits model. How control, mirroring, and simulation can enable imitation and mind reading," *Interdisciplines: What Do Mirror Neurons Mean?: Mirror Systems, Social Understanding and Social Cognition*, www.interdisciplines.org/mirror/papers/5.

Huxley, A. (1932) *Brave New World*, Garden City, New York: Doubleday, Doran.

—— (1954) *The Doors of Perception*, New York: Harper.

Iacoboni, M., Molnar-Szakacs, I., Gallese, V., Buccino, G., and Mazziotta, J. C. (2005) "Grasping the Intentions of Others with One's Own Mirror Neuron System," *PLOS Biology*, Vol. 3, Issue 3, March, 0529–0535. www.plosbiology.org.

Jacob, P. and Jeannerod, M. (2006) "The Motor Theory of Social Cognition. A Critique," *Interdisciplines: What Do Mirror Neurons Mean?: Mirror Systems, Social Understanding and Social Cognition*, www.interdisciplines.org/mirror/papers/2.

Kagan, J. (2001) "Biological Constraint, Cultural Variety, and Psychological Structures," in A. Damasio, A. Harrington, J. Kagan, B. S. McEwen, H. Moss, and R. Shaikh (eds) *Unity of Knowledge: The Convergence of Natural and Human Science*, New York: The New York Academy of Sciences, Vol. 935, 177–190.

Kandel, E. R. and Squire, L. R. (2001) "Neuroscience: Breaking Down Scientific Barriers to the Study of Brain and Mind," in A. Damasio, A. Harrington, J. Kagan, B. S. McEwen, H. Moss, and R. Shaikh (eds) *Unity of Knowledge: The Convergence of Natural and Human Science*, New York: The New York Academy of Sciences, Vol. 935, 118–135.

Kataev, V. (2002) *If Only We Could Know!: An Interpretation of Chekhov*, trans. and ed. H. Pitcher, Chicago: Ivan R Dee.

Knebel', M. (1981) *O deistvennom analize p'ecy i roli*, Moscow: Iskusstvo.

Koch, C. (2005) *The Quest for Consciousness*, New York: Roberts.

Konijn, E. A. (1997) *Acting Emotions: Shaping Emotions on Stage*, trans. B. Leach with D. Chambers, Amsterdam: Amsterdam University Press.

—— (2nd edn 2002) "The Actor's Emotions Reconsidered: A psychological task-based perspective," in P. Zarilli (ed.) *Acting (Re)Considered: A Theoretical and Practical Guide*, New York: Routledge, 62–81.

Lakoff, G. and Johnson, M. (1980) *Metaphors We Live By*, Chicago: University of Chicago Press.

—— (1999) *Philosophy in the Flesh: The Embodied Mind and Its Challenge to Western Thought*, New York: Basic Books.

LeDoux, J. (1996) *The Emotional Brain*, New York: Simon and Schuster.

—— (2002) *Synaptic Self: How Our Brains Become Who We Are*, New York: Penguin Books.

——, Debiec, J., and Moss, H. (eds) (2003) *The Self: From Soul to Brain. Annals of the New York Academy of Sciences*, Vol. 1001, New York: The New York Academy of Sciences.

Levinson, S. C. (2003) *Space in Language and Cognition: Explorations in Cognitive Diversity*, New York: Cambridge University Press.

Lewis, R. (1958) *Method—or Madness?* New York: Samuel French.

—— (1980) *Advice to the Players*, New York: Theatre Communications Group.

Libet, B. (2004) *Mind Time: The Temporal Factor in Consciousness*, Cambridge, Massachusetts: Harvard University Press.

Linklater, Kristin (1976) *Freeing the Natural Voice*, New York: Drama Book Specialists.

Locy, E. (2003) Phone interview, 20 August.

Luria, A. R. (1968) *The Mind of a Mnemonist*, trans. L. Solotaroff, New York: Basic Books.

—— (1976) *The Neurophysiology of Memory*, trans. B. Haigh, New York: John Wiley.

—— (1982) *Language and Cognition*, ed. J. V. Wertsch, New York: John Wiley.

Mazzoni, G. and Nelson, T. O. (eds) (1998) *Metacognition and Cognitive Neuropsychology: Monitoring and Control Processes*, Mahwah, New Jersey: Lawrence Erlbaum Associates.

Meisner, S. and Longwell, D. (1987) *Sanford Meisner on Acting*, New York: Vintage Books.

Meyerhold, V. (1969) *Meyerhold on Theatre*, trans. and ed. E. Braun, New York: Hill and Wang.

Milner, A. D. (ed.) (1998) *Comparative Neuropsychology*, New York: Oxford University Press.

Moss, H. (2003) "Implicit Selves: A Review of the Conference," in J. LeDoux, J. Debiec, and H. Moss (eds) *The Self: From Soul to Brain*, New York: The New York Academy of Sciences, Vol. 1001, 1–30.

Munk, E. (ed.) (1967) *Stanislavski and America*, New York: Hill and Wang.

Parks, S. (1998) *Venus*, New York: Dramatists Play Service.

Pavlov, I. P. (1927) *Conditioned Reflexes: An Investigation of the Physiological Activity in the Cerebral Cortex*, trans. and ed. G. V. Anrep, London: Oxford University Press.

Phelan, P. and Lane, J. (eds) (1998) *The Ends of Performance*, New York: New York University Press.

Pinker, S. (1994) *The Language Instinct*, New York: William Morrow.

—— (1997) *How the Mind Works*, New York: W. W. Norton.

Posner, M. I., Rothbart, M. K., and Gerardi-Caulton, G. (2001) "Exploring the Biology of Socialization," in A. Damasio, A. Harrington, J. Kagan, B. S. McEwen, H. Moss, and R. Shaikh (eds), *Unity of Knowledge: The Convergence of Natural and Human Science*, New York: The New York Academy of Sciences, Vol. 935, 208–216.

Ramachandran, V. S. (2000) "Mirror neurons and imitation learning as the driving force behind 'the great leap forward' in human evolution," *Edge*, no. 60, 29 May, www.edge.org/3rd_culture/ramachandran/ramachandran_p1.html.

—— (2004) *A Brief Tour of Human Consciousness: From Imposter Poodles to Purple Numbers*, New York: Pi Press.

—— (2006) "Mirror Neurons and the Brain in the Vat," *EDGE: The Third Culture*. 1 January, www.edge.org/3rd_culture/ramachandran06/ramachandran06_index.html.

—— and Blakeslee, S. (1998) *Phantoms in the Brain: Probing the Mysteries of the Human Mind*, New York: William Morrow.

—— and Hubbard, E. M. (2003) "Hearing Colors, Tasting Shapes," *Scientific American*, May, 53–59.

Ribot, T. (1884) *Les Maladies de la Volonté*.

—— (1885) *Les Maladies de la Mémoire*.

—— (1897) *The Psychology of Emotions*, ed. H. Ellis, London: Walter Scott.

Riley, S. R. (2004) "Embodied Perceptual Practices: Towards an Embrained and Embodied Model of Mind for Use in Actor Training and Rehearsal," *Theatre Topics* 14:2, 445–469.

Rix, R. (1993) "ALBA EMOTING: A Preliminary Experiment with Emotional Effector Patterns," *Theatre Topics* 3:2, 139–146.

—— (1998) "Learning Alba Emoting," *Theatre Topics* 8:1, 55–72.

Roach, J. R. (1993) *The Player's Passion: Studies in the Science of Acting*, Ann Arbor: The University of Michigan Press.

—— (2004) "It," *Theatre Journal*, Vol. 56, No. 4, 555–568.

Rodenburg, P. (1997) *The Actor Speaks: Voice and the Performer*, London: Methuen.

Rotté, J. (2002) *Acting with Adler*, New York: Limelight Editions.

Sacks, O. (2004) "In the River of Consciousness," *The New York Review of Books*, 15 January, www.nybookscom.

Saussure, F. (1916) *Cours de linguistique generale*.

Schechner, R. (1985) *Between Theater and Anthropology*, Philadelphia: University of Pennsylvania Press.

—— (2002) *Performance Studies: An Introduction*, New York: Routledge.

Searle, J. R. (1992) *The Rediscovery of Mind*, Cambridge, Massachusetts: The MIT Press.

—— (2005) "Consciousness: What We Still Don't Know," *The New York Review of Books*, 23 January, 36–39.

Senelick, L. (1997) *The Chekhov Century: A Century of the Plays in Performance*, New York: Cambridge University Press.

—— (2000) "Chekhov's Plays in English," *North American Chekhov Society Newsletter* (Spring), 11–14.

Shakespeare, W. (1958) *Hamlet*, New York: Pocket Books.

Solso, R. L. (1997) *Mind and Brain Sciences in the 21st Century*, Cambridge, Massachusetts: The MIT Press.

Stanislavski, C. (1926, 1948) *My Life in Art*, trans. J. J. Robbins, New York: Theatre Arts Books.

—— (1936) *An Actor Prepares*, trans. E. R. Hapgood, New York: Routledge.

—— (1949) *Building a Character*, trans. E. R. Hapgood, New York: Routledge.

—— (1951) *Rabota aktëra nad soboi, chasti I & II*. Moscow: Iskusstvo.

—— (1961) *Creating a Role*, trans. E. R. Hapgood, New York: Routledge.

—— (1987) *Stanislavskii repetiruet: zapici i stenogrammy repetitsii*. Moscow: Soyuz Teatral'nyx Deyatelyi, 1987.

Stein, N. L., Ornstein, P. A., Tversky, B., and Brainerd, C. (eds) (1997) *Memory for Everyday and Emotional Events*, Mahwah, New Jersey: Lawrence Erlbaum Associates.

Stoppard, T. (1968) *The Real Inspector Hound*, New York: Samuel French.

Strasberg, L. (1965) *Strasberg at the Actors Studio*, ed. R. H. Hethmon, New York: Theatre Communications Group.

—— (1988) *A Dream of Passion*, London: Bloomsbury.

Suzuki, T. (1896) *The Way of Acting: The Theatre Writings of Tadashi Suzuki*, trans. J. T. Rimer, New York: Theatre Communications Group.

Taylor, F. (1911) *The Principles of Scientific Management*.

Toporkov, V. O. (1998) *Stanislavski in Rehearsal: The Final Years*, trans. C. Edwards, New York: Routledge.

Turner, V. (1982) *From Ritual to Theatre: The Human Seriousness of Play*, New York: Performing Arts Journal Publications.

Wernicke, C. (1874) *Der Aphasische Symptomencomplex*, Breslau: Cohn and Weigert.

Wertenbaker, T. (1996) *Our Country's Good. Plays One*, London: Faber & Faber.

Whitman, W. (1975) *The Complete Poems*, ed. F. Murphy, New York: Penguin Books.

Williams, T. (1997) *The Notebook of Trigorin: A Free Adaptation of Anton Chekhov's The Sea Gull*, New York: New Directions.

Wilson, E. (1998) *Neural Geographies: Feminism and the Microstructure of Cognition*, New York: Routledge.

www.albaemotingha.org. ?

Zarrilli, P. B. (ed.) (2nd edn 2002) *Acting (Re)Considered: A Theoretical and Practical Guide*, New York: Routledge.

Zeki, S. (1999) *Inner Vision: An Exploration of Art and the Brain*, New York: Oxford University Press.

Index

Science and the Stanislavsky Tradition of Acting

Jonathan Pitches

Providing new insight into the well-known tradition of acting, *Science and the Stanislavsky Tradition of Acting* is the first book to contextualise the Stanislavsky tradition with reference to parallel developments in science. Rooted in practice, it presents an alternative perspective based on philosophy, physics, romantic science and theories of industrial management.

Working from historical and archive material, as well as practical sources, Jonathan Pitches traces an evolutionary journey of actor training from the roots of the Russian tradition, Konstantin Stanislavsky, to the contemporary Muscovite director, Anatoly Vasiliev. The book explores two key developments that emerge from Stanislavsky's system – one linear, rational and empirical, while the other is fluid, organic and intuitive. The otherwise highly contrasting acting theories of Vsevolod Meyerhold (biomechanics) and Lee Strasberg (the Method) are dealt with under the banner of the rational or Newtonian paradigm; Michael Chekov's acting technique and the little known ideas of Anatoly Vasiliev form the centrepiece of the other Romantic, organic strain of practice.

Science and the Stanislavsky Tradition of Acting opens up the theatre laboratories of five major practitioners in the twentieth and twenty-first centuries and scrutinises their acting methodologies from a scientific perspective.

ISBN13: 978–0–415–32907–1 (hbk)

Konstantin Stanislavsky

Routledge Performance Practitioners series

Bella Merlin

All books in the *Routledge Performance Practitioners* series are carefully designed to enable the reader to understand the work of a key practitioner. They provide the first step towards critical understanding and a springboard for further study for students on twentieth century, contemporary theatre and theatre history courses.

Stanislavsky, undisputed pioneer of modern acting technique, continues to form the backbone of much drama teaching, actor training and theatre practice. Yet many of his ideas remain either elusive or misunderstood.

This concise and readable book assesses and explains:

- his influence and life history
- ground plans and theatre direction plans
- his widely read text *An Actor Prepares*.

It also gives both a detailed commentary on the key 1898 production of *The Seagull* and an indispensable set of practical exercises for actors, teachers and directors. It will prove invaluable for readers new to Stanislavsky while also giving some fascinating new insights to those familiar with his work.

ISBN13: 978–0–415–25885–2 (hbk)
ISBN13: 978–0–415–25886–9 (pbk)

My Life in Art

Konstantin Stanislavski

Translated by Jean Benedetti

Now, for the first time, translator Jean Benedetti brings us
Stanislavski's complete unabridged autobiography as the author
himself wanted it – from his re-edited 1926 version. The text, in
clear and lively English, is supplemented by a wealth of photos
and illustrations, many previously unpublished.

Konstantin Sergeyevich Stanislavski transformed theatre in the
West with his contributions to the birth of Realist theatre and
unprecedented approach to acting tuition. He established the
Moscow Art Theatre in 1898 with, among other plays, the
premiere of Chekhov's *The Seagull*.

Having survived revolutions, lost his fortune, found fame in
America, and despite being ill and housebound, Stanislavski
continued to write and teach into the 1930s, gaining recognition as
a pivotal figure both in Russia and the US, and one whose
contribution to the arts has endured into the 21st Century.

ISBN13: 978–0–415–43657–1 (hbk)

An Actor's Work

Konstantin Stanislavski

Translated by Jean Benedetti

. . . a far more authentic Stanislavsky . . . a valuable new translation, which is fuller
and more readable than anything else previously attempted.

Laurence Senelick, Tufts University, Boston

Scrupulously precise; combines the deep knowledge and the precision of a scholar
with the pleasant, lively, concise style of a practitioner.

Marie-Christine Autant-Mathieu, Centre National
de la Recherche Scientifique, Paris

Stanislavski's 'system' has dominated actor-training in America since
his writings were first translated into English in the 1920s and '30s.
His systematic attempt to outline a psycho-physical acting technique
single-handedly revolutionized standards of acting in the theatre and
influenced everyone from Marlon Brando to Sean Penn.

His books *An Actor Prepares* and *Building a Character* – originally
conceived as a single volume to encompass both the physical and
psychological aspects of the system – are essential to young actors,
but until now, readers and students have had to contend with
inaccurate, misleading and unwieldy English-language versions.
Some of the mistranslations have resulted in profound distortions in
the way that the system has been interpreted and taught.

At last, Jean Benedetti has succeeded in translating Stanislavski's
huge manual into a lively, fascinating and accurate text in English. He
has remained faithful to the author's original intentions, capturing
Stanislavski's colloquial style making it both contemporary and easy-
to-read for today's actors.

The result – which includes three chapters never before published
in English – is a major contribution to the theatre, and a service to one
of the great innovators of the twentieth century.

ISBN13: 978–0–415–42223–9 (hbk)

RELATED TITLES FROM ROUTLEDGE

Twentieth-Century Actor Training
Edited by Alison Hodge

A uniquely valuable introduction to the life, principles, and practices of fourteen of the most important figures in twentieth century actor training.

Phillip Zarilli; director, actor trainer and actor

Actor training is arguably the central phenomenon of twentieth century theatre making. Here, for the first time, the theories, training exercises and productions of fourteen directors are analysed in a single volume, each one written by a leading expert.

The practitioners included are:

- Stella Adler
- Bertolt Brecht
- Joseph Chaikin
- Jacques Copeau
- Joan Littlewood
- Vsevelod Meyerhold
- Konstantin Stanislavsky

- Eugenio Barba
- Peter Brook
- Michael Chekhov
- Jerzy Grotowski
- Sanford Meisner
- Wlodimierz Staniewski
- Lee Strasbourg

Each chapter provides a unique account of specific training exercises and an analysis of their relationship to the practitioners' theoretical and aesthetic concerns. The collection examines the relationship between actor training and production and considers how directly the actor training relates to performance.

With detailed accounts of the principles, exercises and their application to many of the landmark productions of the past hundred years, this book will be invaluable to students, teachers, practitioners, and academics alike.

ISBN13: 978–0–415–19451–8 (hbk)
ISBN13: 978–0–415–19452–5 (pbk)

Available at all good bookshops
For ordering and further information please visit:
www.routledge.com

Acting (Re)Considered:
A Theoretical and Practical Guide
2nd Edition
(Worlds of Performance)
Edited by Phillip Zarrilli

Acting (Re)Considered is a challenging and extraordinarily eye-opening collection of seminal essays about intercultural theories of acting, training and the actor's body in performance. *Acting (Re)Considered* is an essential part of every theatre student's repertoire, whether they are studying the history, the theory, or the practice of acting.

Included are discussions on acting by or about most of the major figures that have shaped twentieth-century performance, such as:

- Meyerhold
- Copeau
- Decroux
- Artaud
- Brecht
- Growtowski

- Barba
- Suzuki
- Fo
- Warrilow
- Rosenthal
- DaFoe

No other volume on acting is as wide-ranging, as comprehensive, or as international as this one. *Acting (Re)Considered* transforms possibilities for teachers and students of acting.

ISBN13: 978–0–415–26299–6 (hbk)
ISBN13: 978–0–415–26300–9 (pbk)